DATE DUE			

HIGHSMITH #45114

Collaborative Inquiry

in Science, Math, and Technology

Dennis Adams
Mary Hamm

HEINEMANN
PORTSMOUTH, NH

Heinemann
A Division of Reed Elsevier Inc.
361 Hanover Street
Portsmouth, NH 03801-3912

Offices and agents throughout the world

Library of Congress Cataloging-in-Publication Data
Adams, Dennis M.
    Collaborative inquiry in science, math, and technology / Dennis Adams, Mary Hamm.
        p.   cm.
    Includes bibliographical references and index.
    ISBN 0-435-07143-2
    1. Science—Study and teaching.   2. Mathematics—Study and teaching.
.3. Engineering—Study and teaching.   4. Group work in education.
    I. Hamm, Mary.   II. Title.
    Q181.A287   1997   97-37156
    507.1—dc21   CIP

Editor: Leigh Peake and Victoria Merecki
Production: Melissa L. Inglis
Cover design: Joni Doherty
Manufacturing: Louise Richardson

Printed in the United States of America on acid-free paper
01 00 99 98   DA   2 3 4 5 6 7 8 9

The scientifically literate person is one who is aware that science, mathematics, and technology are interdependent human enterprises with strengths and limitations; understands the key concepts and principles of science; is familiar with the natural world and recognizes both its diversity and unity; and uses scientific knowledge and ways of thinking for individual and social purposes.
—F. James Rutherford

Contents

Preface

To make math, science, and technology more meaningful to the lives of children requires connecting the curriculum to the questions they ask about the natural world—questions such as: *Why is the sky blue? How far is my house from the school? Was there life on Mars? Are life and beauty inescapable parts of the universe? How do I find what I want on the Internet? What is the consequence of filling every nook and cranny of our lives with communication devices?*

Creative engagement is one of the keys to scientific inquiry and mathematical problem solving. As new landscapes are opened for interpreting the world, it is important to provide occasions for learners to construct their own knowledge without rigid subject matter restraints. Therefore, we believe that integrating science and mathematics instruction in a cooperative learning–styled classroom is the best way to involve students in active, participatory, and connected learning. Since technology is such an important part of the process, this book also gives some attention to the myths and possibilities surrounding that topic.

Neither science nor mathematics is built on a narrow accumulation of isolated facts. Integration is consistent with students' developing thought processes and with the nature of both subjects. In addition, it is logical to combine these two areas with technology when overlapping areas are best examined by using tools similar to those used by scientists and mathematicians. The idea is to invite students to inquire, discover concepts, and explore the connections collaboratively between science, math, and the natural world.

This book is written in an accessible style that we hope appeals to classroom teachers and those hoping to become teachers. Although most of the concepts provided here are based on the research and the literature, we try to avoid an academic journal approach that breaks up the narrative with countless references and a text that is not interesting to a general audience. As Nathaniel Hawthorne said, easy reading is hard writing.[1]

Collaborative Inquiry in Science, Math, and Technology is designed to support national subject matter standards and enrich the local curriculum already in place in many states. We bring a constructivist approach to the task that is based on the view that knowledge cannot be gained simply by absorbing content through the senses; it requires building on personal experience to think and actually do things. As the new standards suggest, it is also important to take into account the world outside of school when considering how to influence student achievement in science, mathematics, and technology. Along with exploring issues, trends, and standards, this book makes suggestions for implementing learning strategies that capitalize on how children learn best. In the process we hope to challenge your thinking and further stimulate your interest in teaching science and mathematics.

Note

1. Attributed to Nathaniel Hawthorne by Maya Angeleou during a poetry reading in March of 1997.

Chapter One

Cooperative Learning in Elementary Science, Mathematics, and Technology

> *It is through the beauty of personal and group discovery that one proceeds to self-reliant learning, deep knowledge, and freedom.*
> —Friedrich Schiller, *Aesthetic Education of Man*

Cooperative learning is a method of scientific inquiry and mathematical problem solving that allows students to observe phenomena and understand the realities of the universe. This learning is done collectively, as a cohesive, symbiotic group in which ideas and strengths are shared, and problems and questions become tools for discovery. Unfortunately, cooperative learning is often praised more than it is practiced. And despite the accolades, it is frequently misunderstood. Cooperative learning is more than simple group activities or projects for which students have to cooperate to complete their assignments. Teachers using cooperative learning in the classroom have children work in small mixed-ability groups, where they take responsibility for themselves and for each other. This creates a dynamic that requires the development of certain academic and social skills, which in turn supports the cooperative process: These skills are not innate; they are learned.

1

When understood and practiced in an efficient and effective manner, cooperative learning can become a powerful approach to mathematical and scientific inquiry and learning. The value of this approach is considerable, and is realized both in the group setting and in the students as individuals. As Vygotsky writes, "The speech structures mastered by the child become the basic structures of his thinking: What the child can do in cooperation today he can do alone tomorrow" (Dixon-Krauss 1996, p. 115; Vygotsky 1962, p. 104). The approach is deliberate: In many instances, each member of the group is assigned a specific function that is necessary for the successful completion of the group's task. Group achievement depends on individual learning and success. The process is closely monitored: There are provisions for individual accountability and feedback from peers and the teacher. As each person brings his or her unique spirit to the collaborative process, the group takes on enough power to illuminate the consequences of alternative courses of action, and thereby increase and evaluate their options.

Being able to deal collaboratively with the more difficult and uncertain aspects of decision making is important to understanding, predicting, and learning. Since there is more than enough ambiguity in the natural world, it is best for both teachers and students to have alternative possibilities and skills available so that they can modify their applications to fit particular situations. Students learn not to fear the unknown or the uncertain. It is, after all, within these areas of ambiguity that learning occurs. As William James has suggested, both thinking and collaboration requires that learners expect uncertainty and leave room for it. He writes: "We need to restore the vague to its proper place in our mental life" (James 1909). Learning within a small circle of peers can help students navigate around the seemingly difficult clutter of uncertainty, and aspire to things that had previously exceeded their grasp. Working in a community with others is an effective way for students to gain the confidence and ability to see what *can be*, even though it *isn't yet*.

A Shared Sense of Community

One of the main reasons that cooperative, small-group learning has become so popular is because it motivates and academically engages students within a social setting. It is a good way for three or four children of mixed backgrounds and capabilities to form productive friendships with each other as they work toward a common goal. This has been shown to increase each child's self-esteem and academic achievement (Slavin 1990). The essential elements for cooperative learning include: positive interdependence, face-to-face interaction, personal responsibility, interpersonal skill development, and group processing. Scientific, mathematical, and technological instruction can be enhanced with procedures for expanding cooperative groups and mixed-ability learning teams, so that teachers can make effective use of this instructional approach.

Cooperative learning involves working together to accomplish shared goals that are beneficial to individuals and the group. Students are able to learn together and perform alone in an environment that allows them to construct knowledge actively. In the cooperative classroom communal responsibility and civic engagement are not viewed as optional extras: Everyone is involved and cooperation becomes part of the fabric of instruction. The collaborative spirit can influence schooling at every level. Building team-based organizational structures in the classroom can, for example, make it easier for teachers to reach out beyond their classroom and contribute to their colleagues' success.

A common element in successful schools is a shared sense of community and a socially integrated sense of purpose. Shared common interests and common ground make for more civil and intelligent discussions than when all the attention is on individual choice and unconditional rights. When there is no limit on individual self-realization, public spaces decay and civic culture is weakened. Schools, like the community in general, need common spaces where people meet and share a life in common. From civic conversation across group lines to a more collegial school staff, cooperative learning can create a lasting and meaningful contribution.

Cooperative learning is more than having students cooperate in a group activity or project. There is a set of strategies that encourage student cooperation while learning in a variety of settings, disciplines, and different grade levels. The process involves promoting positive interdependence by dividing the work load, providing joint rewards, holding individuals accountable, and getting students actively involved in helping each other master the topic being studied. Creative social engagement is paramount.

Cooperative learning is one successful element of educational reform. The whole language movement recognized its benefits and embraced it early on. In 1996 the National Science Teachers Association's (NSTA) publication *Pathways* encouraged its use in implementing the new national standards in science education. It has solid teacher support and a favorable research base. Researchers have also commented on how cooperative learning improves problem-solving skills in mathematics and attitudes toward inquiry-based scientific instruction (Tobin 1990). More and more teachers are incorporating the concept of group work (with individual accountability) into their classrooms, and it is becoming common to see suggestions for active team learning across the curriculum.

Cooperative learning has permeated the standards projects and teacher training from the preservice to the inservice level. The National Council for the Teachers of Mathematics's (NCTM) mathematics standards fall into four broad categories: problem solving, communication, reasoning, and mathematical connections. All of the categories leave space for collaboration. In addition, cooperative learning is one of several approaches and methods that have been consistently supported by the research on science and mathematics teaching (Davidson 1990). As teachers learn when and how to design instruction cooperatively, the process transforms itself from a hot new method into a routine part of a good instructional program.

Cooperative learning must be fashioned with a sensitivity as to how students connect content areas and relate scientific/mathematical/technological ideas together. With students this means working in pairs or small, mixed-ability groups to help each other learn. Through group work students learn to take more responsibility for their own learning. There is a growing consensus that active team learning enriches the science and mathematics curriculum. Circumstantial evidence suggests that it can also help foster cooperative relationships among teachers, administrators, and parents. More than other innovations, cooperative learning can change the school climate by encouraging cooperation, cohesion, and teamwork.

Heterogeneous Grouping

Students seem to find cooperative learning activities more satisfying and useful than traditional settings. Fields (1988) suggests that cooperative learning fosters social skills, positive peer relationships, and higher levels of self-esteem in all students. As learning teams discuss science and mathematics, students construct meaning by jointly working on solutions to problems, raising original problems, and exchanging ideas. In the process, scientific, mathematical, and technological applications can come alive as student teams connect the concepts being studied to their everyday experiences.

Cooperative learning strategies promote language skills along with subject matter. Group study offers students many opportunities to improve speaking skills and use language to inquire about and communicate findings. This is particularly important for children who are not assertive and for those whose second language is English. As students show more willingness to interact with others, there are more significant cross-cultural friendships formed and more acceptance of students with disabilities (Savage 1994; Sharan and Shachar 1988).

Students who work together in mixed-ability groups are also more likely to develop mixed racial and ethnic acquaintances and friendships. As heterogeneously grouped students cooperate to reach a common goal, they learn to appreciate and respect each other (Barba 1995). In addition to fostering positive interpersonal relationships, research indicates that the use of cooperative learning or cross-age groups increases students' science concept acquisition (Ramirez and Castanada 1994). This same study suggests that when culturally diverse students work in collaborative groups, their attitudes toward science and math improve.

Research with minority students has shown that many of them prefer peer tutoring in small groups. Peer tutoring is also an effective way of bridging linguistic barriers for bilingual and bicultural students (Watson 1991). The self-esteem of girls at the middle school level increased through use of cooperative academic activities (Cohen, Lotan, and Catanzarite 1990). Through this research it becomes clear that cooperative learning allows minorities and young women to make more significant academic gains than in traditional settings (Barba 1995).

Getting Teamwork Started in the Classroom

Getting started with cooperative learning in math and science means defining classroom responsibilities, goals, policies, and procedures; it means departing from the archetypal math and science classrooms of the past, and allowing the cooperative classroom to develop and take shape. Cooperative learning will not take place with students sitting in rows facing the teacher. Collaboration will not occur in a classroom where students must raise their hand to talk or move away from their desk. Responsible behavior is part and parcel to cooperative learning, and needs to be developed and encouraged. Authoritarian approaches to discipline will not work if we are expecting students to be responsible for their own learning and behavior; however, this does not preclude instructing students on how to work together in ways that support the cooperative approach. Learners must be taught to consider other groups working around them, the noise level, and so forth.

Establishing a cooperative math and science classroom requires organizing the classroom so that it is easier for students to develop and practice group process skills. Changing the classroom organization so that students are in a supportive environment with face-to-face contact requires changes in the physical structure. Desks must be pushed together in small groups or replaced with tables to facilitate group interaction and to form comfortable work spaces that are conducive to open communication.

In creating two-, three-, four-, or five-member groups it is best to try and organize as heterogeneously as possible. (We suggest not going beyond five students in a group.) If you are forming partnerships (two students) you might consider having the students write down four people with whom they would most like to work. The teacher can then pick partners with the student's interests in mind (students usually get at least their number four choice). Even a small group can mix children by sex, race, ethnic background, and academic ability. Mixed-ability learning groups have proved effective in mathematics and science classes.

After the classroom has been arranged and the groups formed, it is then necessary to establish rules and standards within which the cooperative groups must operate. It is important to involve students in this process. Rules and standards should be kept simple and might include the following:

1. Everyone is responsible for his or her own work.
2. Productive talk is desired, and necessary for learning.
3. Each person is responsible for his or her own behavior.
4. Try to learn from others within your small group.
5. Everyone must be willing to help anyone who asks.
6. Ask the teacher for help if no one in the group can answer the question.

Group roles and individual responsibilities also need to be clearly defined and arranged, so that each group member's contribution is unique and essential, and so that valuable class time is used efficiently. If the learning activities require materials, students may be required to take responsibility for assembling and storing them. Likewise, many exercises require a cleanup period when completed. Tasks such as these should be assigned to members within the group ahead of time, so that each member of the group understands her or his responsibilities and contribution to the group. As learners come to appreciate their place and value within the group, the activities become more effective and the power of cooperative learning grows. Unlike competitive and individualistic goal structures, the operative pronoun in cooperative learning is *we* not *me*.

Problem Solving in the Cooperative Learning Classroom

In cooperative learning classrooms, teachers provide time for students to grapple with problems, try out strategies, discuss, experiment, explore, and evaluate. The national science and mathematics standards encourage teachers to put students in small groups in which they can argue about key concepts and work on problems as a team. The primary focus is on the students' investigations, discussions, and group projects. Whatever variation of cooperative learning a teacher chooses, students are given opportunities to integrate their learning through interactive discovery experiences and applying their collaborative problem-solving skills. In addition, any approach to cooperative learning should incorporate group goals, individual accountability, and an equal opportunity for all group members to achieve success. It is more important to emphasize the reasoning involved in working on a problem than getting the answer.

When the initial activity or problem solving is over, students need to spend time reflecting on group work. A basic question for students to ask is: *What worked well and how might the process be improved?* Students and teachers need to be involved in evaluating learning and the cooperative group environment. The learning climate is particularly important: It strongly influences such things as self-esteem, motivation, discipline, and expression—as well as individual and group achievement. At the end of an investigation the teacher can develop more class unity by pointing out how each small-group research effort contributes to the class goal of understanding and exploring a topic.

Teaching the Cooperative Group Lesson

In order for cooperative learning in math and science classrooms to be effective and engaging, it is important that students are well grounded before the group work begins. During the initial introduction of the lesson, the teacher can help students understand the problem and establish guidelines for the group's work. The teacher should present or review necessary concepts and skills with the whole class, and offer a part of the problem or an example of a similar problem for the class to try. Opportunities for discussion should be provided, questions should be encouraged, and solutions should come from the students whenever possible. After this initial warm-up period, the actual group problem is then presented. The class is encouraged to discuss and clarify the problem or task. Before breaking the class into groups it is helpful to have a student (or two) explain the problem that the teacher has presented to the class, in the student's own words. This allows for a broadening of interpretation and a cooperative approach to the problem. It also offers the teacher an opportunity to clear up misunderstandings before the entire class begins working. The learners should then break up into their designated groups.

As students continue to work cooperatively to solve the problem, the teacher can observe, listen to the groups' ideas, and offer assistance as needed. The teacher should be prepared to provide extended activities if a group finishes early. If a group is having difficulties, the teacher can help by asking them what they know or have learned so far, or perhaps point out a misconception or error in reasoning that may be inhibiting the group's progress. Sometimes a group has trouble getting along or focusing on what they are supposed to be doing. At this time it may be necessary to refocus the group's attention by asking questions such as: *What are you supposed to be doing? What is the task? How will you get organized? What materials do you need? Who will do what?*

After the group work is completed, students again meet as a class to summarize and share their findings, processes, and solutions. Students should be encouraged to discuss what worked and what did not. As this exchange of information takes place, the teacher can utilize this opportunity to extend the cooperative learning process across the class—to the benefit of all students, successful and otherwise—by asking questions such as: *How did you organize the task? What problems did you have? What method did you use? Was your group method effective? Did anyone have a different method or strategy for solving the problem? Do you think your solution makes sense? What other problem does this remind you of?*

Students are encouraged to listen and respond to other students' comments; they should be encouraged to generalize from their results. It is also helpful to make notes of the responses on the chalkboard to help summarize the class data at the close of the lesson.

Developing a Cooperative Perspective Means Changing Attitudes

The teaching and learning methods that teachers choose to use convey implicit messages to students about what is valued and important. If the bulk of classroom time is used having students listen to the teacher or working on isolated paper-and-pencil tasks usually found in textbooks or practice sheets, then the underlying message conveyed to students is that learning means mastering a narrow range of unconnected skills and emphasizing product.

Competition anxiety, product-oriented thinking skills, and lack of problem-solving abilities have been identified as problems that inhibit a child's development. Schools have traditionally been competitive institutions, with increased emphasis on competition as students move up through the system. The messages sent to students through this model is that quick, *right* answers—usually drawn from short-term memory—are valued. Children learn to depend on the faster students to provide answers and on the teacher to validate their thinking. When students focus on completing assignments quickly, they rarely stop to question the reasonableness of their response or the meaning behind it. Such pedagogical techniques not only inhibit students' self-reliance, they do little to produce an understanding of science and mathematics.

Research suggests that levels of anxiety significantly inhibit achievement (Bulmahn and Young 1982). When a competitive structure is bonded to an abstract style of presentation, anxiety levels increase, causing some students to withdraw into themselves. Cooperative learning attempts to deal with these educational detriments by maximizing interaction and changing what is valued in the learning process. The result can be classrooms in which more productive learning is possible.

When students work in collaborative groups, they have a better chance to explore ideas, justify their views, and synthesize knowledge within a supportive environment. Instead of forcing students to become quiet, isolated workers who are reluctant to share answers, shielding their papers from other students' eyes, students are encouraged to share ideas, collaborate, and pool their knowledge to solve or perhaps resolve a problem. Learning is more cooperative and less competitive.

Many professional associations have suggested an emphasis on group learning that relies on reason rather than rote. The American Association for the Advancement of Science, for example, has called for a collaborative common core of learning that stresses thinking skills instead of memorization of details. One of the key features of cooperative learning is that students pool critical thinking, giving and receiving help in a learning environment where it is safe to make mistakes—and learn from those mistakes.

In a collaborative setting the teacher helps students gain confidence in their own ability and the group's ability to work through problems, and consequently rely less on the teacher as the sole source of knowledge. Students are motivated by social contact with their peers and their sense of achievement as they succeed in dealing with challenging tasks through the group effort, rather than through strict, step-by-step teacher direction.

Both teachers and students must undergo a major shift in values and attitudes if a collaborative learning environment is to succeed. The traditional school experience has taught many students that the teacher is there to validate their thinking and direct learning. Since first entering school, children are compared with one another for recognition. Unlearning these dated structures takes time. Students used to traditional classrooms will need time to adjust to group work and decision making.

Likewise, students in cooperative learning settings often raise questions and ideas that go beyond the teacher's guidebook. To keep up to date teachers must also continue being learners and become comfortable with saying *I don't know* or *Let's find out*, as students push them in new learning directions that are unimagined and unplanned. Cooperative classroom environments require teachers who actively seek to create them. When they do, many teachers will find that their best instincts about group work are confirmed.

Attitudes change as students learn to work cooperatively, rather than taking individual ownership of ideas. It is important that students understand that simply telling an answer or doing someone's work is not helping a classmate learn. Learning involves asking the right questions to help someone grasp the meaning, or explaining with an example. These understandings need to be actively and clearly explained, demonstrated, and developed by the teacher. As students share information many find time for reflection and assessment—instead of rushing to finish a task. Small groups can write collective stories, edit each others writing, solve mathematical problems, correct homework, prepare for tests, investigate science questions, examine artifacts, work on a computer simulation, brainstorm an invention, create a sculpture, or arrange a new rap music tune.

Another benefit of cooperative learning is that students are provided with group stimulation and support. The small group provides safe opportunities for trial and error, and a safe environment for asking questions or expressing opinions. More students get chances to respond, raise ideas, or ask questions. As each student brings unique strengths and experiences to the group and contributes to the process, respect for individual differences is enhanced.

The group also acts as a motivator. Many times ideas are pushed beyond what an individual would attempt or suggest. The quality and quantity of thinking increases as more ideas are added, surpassing what the individual could do alone. Group interaction enhances idea development and students have many opportunities to be teachers as well as learners. Simultaneously, the small-group structure extends children's resources as they are encouraged to pool strategies and share information. More withdrawn students become more active. Students who often have a hard time sticking to a task receive group assistance so they can learn to monitor their time better and become a productive member of the group. The unity of the group has been found to extend beyond the classroom, to the playground and social situations (Adams and Hamm 1989).

Dividing the class into groups changes the complexion of the classroom. The teacher has six or eight groups instead of twenty-five to thirty-five individuals with which to make good contact each day. In addition, with a cooperative learning approach there are twenty-five to thirty-five aides in the classroom. Students monitor each other while creating a spirit of cooperation and helpfulness. Students become better listeners within a cooperative structure, and must collectively agree to ask for help so that they ask better questions and are more eager for teacher input.

Cooperative learning can help teachers spend less time policing the class, as students learn they are capable of validating their own values and ideas. Teachers are freer to move about, work with small groups, and interact in a more personal manner with students. Cooperative group learning can also be arranged so there is less paperwork for the teacher. Reviewing six or eight group papers usually requires less time and effort than twenty or thirty.

It usually takes more than one or two tries with cooperative learning to get cooperative groups going. Teachers and students who are not used to active learning teams must be eased into the process through a consistent routine. When high achievers from traditional classrooms have to work in a group, they may have initial problems because they are accustomed to being rewarded for quick answers with low levels of thinking. It may take some time for them to become comfortable working cooperatively. Teachers and administrators have to make a conscious effort to move schools away from the competitive factory model. This means going beyond the usual cosmetic effects (which have little positive value) to significant structural changes.

Having good models can help, but major change will require an emphasis on vision. It takes time and practice for the vital energy inherent in new skills to become part of a teacher's repertoire. Teachers need to be actively involved in learning new strategies and goal structures—and they need support while implementing new skills. Change takes time and systematic staff development. Inservice workshops can help provide assistance as teachers try activities, share experiences, and receive feedback within a supportive environment of collaboration. Purposeful collegial meetings may help.

A few carefully and cooperatively structured efforts by a group of teachers can result in positive changes in the organization of the school, the professional life of the teacher, and the instructional program. As students and teachers learn to conduct their communications with collegiality and civility, collaborative teams can help build a broader sense of community and even stimulate collaboration between teachers. Connecting mutual achievement and collegial relationships can be extended to staff meetings, committees, and relationships with parents. Traditional teachers and parents must come to understand that it is sometimes all right for students to share answers.

As students and teachers become participating members of a collegial team of peers, both develop a joint sense of purpose and even more efficiently tap the possibilities of cooperative learning. Method certainly isn't all, but empirical and circumstantial evidence supports the use of cooperative learning techniques in the classroom.

Cooperative Learning: The Reality of Change

Cooperative learning has a large and supportive empirical base at the elementary level, where teachers and students seem to take naturally to it. Cooperative learning activities, group problem solving, and cross-age tutoring are now generally accepted as useful tools for helping students get the most out of inquiry-based science and mathematics in the elementary school. However, the research weakens at the high school and college levels, although attention is now being given to how collaboration can lead to higher level conceptual learning.

Because of its dramatic effect in the elementary grades, cooperative learning may very well be the single most effective way to bring about change in the traditional school environment. The method works best over an extended period of time, but the results are not automatic: It often takes sustained professional development activities to persuade both neophyte and veteran teachers to provide for collaborative small-group alternatives or additions in their current repertoire of teaching methods.

Science and mathematics have always been an interpersonal conversation about reality. Both subjects have a history of changed minds. Science—along with its mathematical and technological associates—has constructed a magnificent and constantly evolving framework for comprehending the physical and biological universe. Being able to put our knowledge to the test and use it to make predictions about reality requires more supportive learning environments that recognize an active role for peers and adults. Active team learning is more than an innovation in itself; it is a catalyst for other changes in curricula, instruction, and schooling. Slavin's research (1990) clearly suggests that becoming a contributing member of a collegial team promotes self-discovery, higher level reasoning, social cohesion, and academic achievement. In cooperative learning, students and teachers are viewed as being rooted in a network of familial and community relationships that make up a civil society. Like an extended family, everyone cares about individual and mutual achievement. Individual rights are *balanced* by reciprocal obligation and mutual interdependence.

By tapping into students' natural curiosity and creating a learning community, students and teachers can use cooperative methods to achieve academic goals. Cooperative learning can be used with confidence across subjects and grade levels to explore meaning and help students care for one another. As students come together in teams they can look at scientific and mathematical issues and jointly ask: *Where can we go with this?* and *How might it make our world better?* By building on the group energy and idealism of students the thinking, learning, and doing processes can be pushed forward. Decades ago it was Vygotsky's contention that children learn by reflecting on and gradually internalizing instructional concepts through interactions with peers and more learned adults. It has taken us some time to figure out that he was right when he said, "What the child can do in cooperation today he can do alone tomorrow" (Vygotsky 1962, p. 104).

A democracy is a community always in the making. Of course the smaller the size of the community, the more personal the relationships and the greater the individual responsibility. Learning to work with others is an important element in developing democratic values *and* in furthering new curricular goals. By creating a learning community where students collaborate to reach meaningful goals, cooperative learning is capable of making a real difference across the curriculum. Even when it doesn't take you all the way to a socially integrating sense of purpose, it helps open the mind to what might be. If we diminish collaborative possibilities we lose something of incalculable value when it comes to accommodating the scientific, mathematical, and technological core of our future. We don't want to look back in a decade and bemoan lost opportunities.

Cooperative Interdisciplinary Activities

Activity Title: Bridge Building

Purpose and Objectives

This is an interdisciplinary science and math activity. Students will reinforce their skills in communication, group process, social studies, language arts, the arts, mathematics, science, and technology.

Materials

- lots of newspaper and masking tape
- one slightly heavy rock
- one small- to medium-size cardboard box

Have students bring in stacks of newspapers. The project will require approximately one foot-high pile of newspapers per small group.

Procedure

Bridges are a tribute to technological efforts that employ community planning, engineering efficiency, mathematical precision, aesthetics, group effort, and construction expertise. For the first part of this activity, divide students into three groups of about four students each. Explain that each group is responsible for investigating one aspect of bridge building. Have each group choose a representative to speak for their group.

Group One—Research and Information—is responsible for going to the library, looking up facts about bridges, and bringing back information to be shared with the class.

Group Two—Aesthetics, Art, and Literature—must discover songs, books, paintings, artwork, and so forth, that deal with bridges and present the group's findings to the class.

Group Three—Measurement and Engineering—must discover design techniques, blueprints, angles, and measurements of actual bridge designs. If possible, visit a local bridge to look at the structural design, in addition to its other attributes. The group must present its findings to the class.

Have the group representatives get together to present their findings to the class. Allow time for questions and discussion.

The second part of this activity involves actual bridge construction by the students. Assemble the collected stacks of newspaper, tape, rock, and the box at the front of the room. Divide the class into groups. Instruct each group to take a newspaper pile and several rolls of masking tape to their area. Explain that the group will be responsible for building a free-standing bridge using only the newspapers and tape. The bridge is to be constructed so that it will support the large rock, and so that the box can pass underneath. Planning is crucial: Give each group ten minutes of planning time, during which they are allowed to talk and plan together. During the planning time remind the students that they are not allowed to touch the newspapers and tape, but encourage them to pick up the rock, make estimates of the height of the box, make a sketch of the bridge, or assign group roles of responsibility.

At the end of the planning time give the students about thirty minutes to build their bridge. Remind them that they may not handle the rock or the box—only the newspapers and tape. A few more minutes may be necessary to ensure that all groups have a chance of getting their constructions to meet at least one of the two tests (rock or box). If a group finishes early, have the members add some artistic flourishes to their bridge or watch the building process in other groups.

Evaluation, Completion, and/or Follow-up
Stop all groups after the allotted time. Survey the bridges with the class and allow each group to try to pass the two tests for their bridge: Does the bridge support the rock and does the box fit underneath? Discuss the design of each bridge and how the bridges compare with the bridges researched earlier. As a follow-up activity, have each group measure its bridge and design a blueprint (include angles, length, and width of the bridge), so that another group could build the bridge by following this model.

Activity Title: Investigate Your Time Line

Purpose and Objectives
This challenging interdisciplinary activity was designed by a preservice teacher for fourth and fifth graders. Students will learn scientific and mathematical concepts of time and measurement as well as the science and math skills of observing, predicting, estimating, measuring, and recording.

Working in groups of four or five, each group makes a time line of the ages of the people in their groups and the events in their lives. Students will compare the events in their lives with other students. Students record and report the results, which will indicate:

- how a time line can show different cultural and ethnic patterns
- how maturity affects decisions
- how time changes students' perceptions of math and science

Materials

- a thirteen-foot-long piece of butcher paper for each group
- rulers
- fine-point markers
- a teacher-prepared time line to post on the board for the students to use as a model

Procedure

Explain that the students will be working in cooperative groups to mark time lines of the ages and lives of the people in their groups. Divide students into groups of four or five students. Have students pass out the materials to each group. Explain your model time line and give students directions for making their own time lines:

Have the students find out the ages of the people in their group—who is the oldest, next oldest, youngest, and so forth. Instruct students to start the time line on January first of the year that the oldest person in the group was born. Tell students to end the time line on the last day of the current year. Have the students use a different color marker to mark off each year and explain that each year equals one foot and an inch equals a month (using thirteen feet of butcher paper assumes that no one is older than twelve years). (To do this activity in an older class, use three inches for a year [instead of one foot] and a quarter inch for a month.) Ask the students to write the important events in their lives at the bottom of each year. Tell the students to make a color key with the colored markers. Each student has his or her own color. Have the students put a dot or star by the important events in their lives, such as birthdays, birth of siblings, and other important events.

Evaluation, Completion, and/or Follow-up

Have a volunteer from each group present the group's time line and post it on the classroom bulletin board.

Activity Title: Data Inventory—Mathematics

Purpose and Objectives

This activity involves primary students in making a collaborative group inventory. Students will learn how to make an inventory and record their data. Groups of two will decide what they want to count and make a list. Students will then tally the number of objects in the classroom and then find the number in each category by counting. The calculator can be used for counting large numbers. This activity should be used with younger students near the end of the year when counting skills are more developed. Students will be involved in several phases: deciding what to count, collecting data, and displaying results.

Materials

- paper
- pencils
- calculators

Procedure

Discuss what an inventory is and why stores take an inventory. Tell children that you want them to help you find out how many different things are in the classroom. Let students decide what they want to count—books, desks, tables, chairs, toys, games, math materials, and so on. Make a list of what they suggest. If students are not used to tallying, take time to introduce the concept. Demonstrate how to record the tally (four strokes down and one across). Stress the accuracy of making a written record. Have two children demonstrate keeping a tally. One points to the object and the other makes a tally mark. Let each child practice with a partner. Have the pair count their tallies. A calculator may be used. Use the constant key or press + 5 = (every time the = key is pressed, another five items will be added).

Evaluation, Completion, and/or Follow-up

Post the inventory counts. Discuss how many of each thing is in the room. Focus on categories such as

- large and small numbers
- numbers more than 100
- the relationship between the amount counted and the size of the objects (for example, children may observe that crayons take less space than books)

Instruct students to take an inventory of their homes, their books, or the vehicles going by on their street in an hour. Let them decide what they want to count. (This activity was adapted from the National Council of Mathematics Curriculum and Evaluation Standards, Addenda Series) (1991).

Activity Title: Water in the Air

Purpose and Objectives

This science and math lesson will help students discover the properties of water using hands-on experiments and observations while working together in small groups.

Materials

- glass bottle
- tumbler
- chalkboard
- 8" x 10" piece of cardboard
- ice
- hot water
- small lamp
- two sponges

Procedure

Have group members do the following: Get two sponges that are the same size and wet them. Make two spots of equal wetness on the chalkboard. Fan one of the spots vigorously with a piece of cardboard.

Question the students about what occurs, then explain that the moisture on the fanned spot will evaporate more quickly because the fanning blows away the saturated air above the spot and provides a fresh supply of unsaturated air.

Have students dip their forefinger into a tumbler of water. Remind students to keep their forefinger and dry middle finger a slight distance apart. Instruct students to blow on both fingers at the same time so that they can experience the cooling effect of evaporation. As water evaporates from the forefinger, the heat needed for evaporation is taken from the finger, making it cooler. The dry finger, which serves as a control, does not become cooler.

Evaluation, Completion, and/or Follow-up

This is a basic activity designed to introduce a theme that includes water, weather, and so forth. See other related activities. Encourage students to explain what happened. They may wish to draw a picture or write a brief explanation.

Activity Title: Seed Hunt

Purpose and Objectives

This activity looks at the tremendous diversity of plants and their seeds. Students will classify seeds and the properties of seeds; describe the categories, verbally and in writing, and their reasons for putting the seeds in those categories; and compare and organize their seeds. Students will work cooperatively together and make predictions (guesses) as to where the seed might be categorized. This activity can be integrated with the data inventory activity mentioned earlier.

Materials

- science/math journal
- brown paper bag
- pencils

Procedure
Introduce the concept of the great variety in plant seeds. Tell students that they're going to go on a seed hunt with a small group of two or three other classmates. Explain that their task is to try to find and collect samples of one seed that fits each of these categories: seeds that float, seeds that blow, seeds that hitchhike, helicopter seeds (or seeds that twirl). Instruct students to record their findings in their science and math journal.

Evaluation, Completion, and/or Follow-up
Have student groups bring their seeds to class to compare their findings and test their guesses with other groups.

Activity Title: What Do You See?

Purpose and Objectives
In this activity students will develop the cooperative inquiry process skills of observing, comparing, measuring, inferring, and recording. Students will be able to observe and record data accurately. Students will use simple scientific equipment. Students will demonstrate the ability to work in groups in an organized and productive manner.

Materials

- five samples: a housefly, a computer disk, a flower, a piece of fabric, and a sample of paper (other samples may be substituted for those listed)
- twelve magnifying glasses
- six rulers
- an observation sheet for each student

Procedure
Establish six stations around the room that include two magnifying glasses, one of the samples, and a ruler. Provide each student with an

observation sheet. Divide the students into six groups of four students each and assign a group to each station. Explain that at each station the group has ten minutes to record as many observations about the sample as possible. Have each student in the group, while using the magnifying glass and the ruler, make an observation for the group to record. Have the students rotate as time allows. As a class, compare and discuss the students' observations.

Evaluation, Completion, and/or Follow-up
Evaluate the data sheets based on organization, observation skills, and accuracy.

Chapter Two

Developing Critical and Creative Thinking and Portfolio Assessment

Imagination is the beginning of creation
You imagine what you desire
You will what you imagine
You create what you will
—George Bernard Shaw, *The Dictionary of Quotable Definitions*

Can the science and mathematics curriculum value critical and creative thinking? As Shaw would suggest, if we can imagine it and gather the strength of will to sustain it, *we can create it*. As pedagogical research evidences and the escalating demands of our technologically burgeoning society indicate, educators *must* incorporate these attributes into the science and mathematics classroom to do justice to the curriculum, and therefore to the *students.* Critical and creative thinking are such an integral part of new directions in analytic problem solving and interdisciplinary inquiry that they are increasingly hard to ignore.

In the inquiry-based science and mathematics classroom the cooperative learning emphasis is on thinking, not telling children what to think. The basic idea is to foster the creative and critical imagination in a community of responsible and reflective learners. Students must be competent thinkers to take part in mathematical and scientific inquiry, and avoid being misled by the logically insupportable. Here we suggest a constructivist approach that builds content understanding on a student's personal experience: Teachers increasingly encourage children to put thinking skills to work analyzing and solving problems that are part of the world in which they live.

New curricular standards and teaching methods pay attention to the world outside of school. One way of doing this is by encouraging student thought processes that are similar to those used by scientists. Scientists collect data, select information, and reflect on what it might mean for the natural world. As students use critical thinking skills to solve problems within such a framework, they are more apt to approach a task in an unconventional, spontaneous, flexible, and original manner. Sometimes this is done within a preexisting paradigm. Sometimes it means breaking out of conventional boundaries. And sometimes, as Wallace Stevens has said, *The truth depends upon a walk around the lake.*

Many influences on thinking are generated far from the scientific and educational world. Popular culture may be an oxymoron, but students who grow up in the nonlinear world of television, computers, and the Internet may have a jump on adults in adapting to the chaotic world of technological change. However, it seems unlikely that they will be as able when it comes to sustaining the more linear aspects of thoughtful inquiry. Will twenty-first-century society place a higher value on length of attention span, the ability to do many things at once, or both?

Critical and Creative Thinking

Critical and creative thinking are constructed by the mind, built on personal experience. Various attributes of thoughtfulness develop along with other elements of functional intelligence and personality. The quality of an individual's thinking is influenced by experiences, culture, emotions, environment, and educational exposure and possibilities. As students learn scientific processes and mathematical problem-solving skills, they increase their reasoning abilities both inductively and deductively.

Being good at thinking means being able to form alternative explanations and demonstrate intellectual curiosity in a manner that is flexible, elaborate, and novel to the thinker. As part of their responsibility to the future, teachers must respect the unique ideas developed by students, and encourage creative and critical thinking. It seems clear that many future problems will be solved by people who are flexible, open, original, and creatively productive. So what students can *actually do* with scientific and mathematical knowledge is of the utmost importance.

Good critical thinking activities encourage students to analyze underlying assumptions that influence meanings and interpretations of information. Such intellectually demanding thinking leads children to identify, clarify, problem solve, and become more productive. The questions explored can be as general as: *Are there limits to how much of the physical universe we can understand?* and *How secure are the foundations of knowledge in science and mathematics?* Questions can also be as specific as: *How did you figure that one out?* or *What does it mean?* The wording may be changed, but children are never too young to analyze the underlying assumptions that influence meanings. And they are never too young to question the interpretation of findings and participate in the act of knowledge creation.

Although teachers often connect the characteristics of critical and creative thinking, there are traditional differences between the two: *Critical thinking* is viewed as reasoning, criticizing, performing logical analyses, searching for supporting evidence, and evaluating outcomes. Activities that support this involve clarifying problems, considering alternatives, strategically planning, problem solving, and analyzing the results. *Creative thinking* is viewed as fluency, flexibility, originality, and elaboration. Skills developed in this area would result in the creation of unique expressions, original conceptions, novel approaches, and demonstrations of the ability to see things in imaginative and unusual ways. Problem solving and implementation are part of both creative and critical thinking.

Multiple Entry Points to Knowledge

Recognizing that thinking skills are directly involved in successful learning throughout the curriculum would not come as a surprise to most teachers. There is, however, a tendency to think of scientific method and mathematics as clear-cut: Students formulate hypotheses, conduct experiments, collect data, analyze the data, and interpret the findings. Working scientists, mathematicians, and engineers will say the reality is far less clear-cut and tidy. There are many false starts and detours as they work through alternatives to discover relationships and invent new perspectives. What makes it satisfying for many scientists is the sheer power of searching at the frontiers of knowledge. This passion for inquiry and new experiences is just as important for students.

Critical and creative thinkers tend to be reflective. They think problems through, have a flexibility to consider original solutions, and a curiosity to pose and expand new questions. Research suggests that giving students multiple perspectives and entry points into subject matter increases thinking and learning (Sears and Marshall 1990). The implication is that ideas about how students learn a subject needs to be pluralized—almost any concept can be approached from multiple directions—while emphasizing understanding and making meaningful connections across subjects. This means making educational alternatives and resources (human and technological) that will appeal to pupils with different learning styles and cultural backgrounds consistently available. Schools need to incorporate frameworks for learning that build on the multiple ways of thinking and representing knowledge. By organizing lessons that respect multiple entry points to knowledge, teachers can enhance thoughtfulness and make the school a home for inquiry.

A student's thinking ability evolves through a dynamic of personal abilities, social values, and academic and out-of-school experiences—all multiple entry points to knowledge. From birth, children are struggling with critical thinking, and are consumed with making sense of their environment. They do this by curiously grappling with the confusing, learning ways of understanding, developing schemes for thinking, and finding meaning. As they enter school, children can sing songs, tell stories, and use their own processes of reasoning and intuiting to understand their surroundings. By the time they reach first grade they have already developed a rich body of knowledge about the world around them. These beginnings can be extended in school when the teacher cultivates a broad disposition to critical thinking throughout the curriculum. Working with natural rhythms is important, but it takes cooperative, learning-centered instruction to continue the process of developing mature thinkers.

Constructivism: Connecting Thinking, Content, and Experience

Constructivism is a learning theory that suggests that knowledge is most effectively acquired by evoking personal meaning in the learner. Although there are differences in terminology, there are many similarities with Piagetian theory. From a constructivist viewpoint, a conceptual knowledge of math and science is constructed by learners over time within a meaningful social setting. This social-constructivist perspective asserts that cooperative interaction with others is an important element in giving all students an opportunity to make sense of what they are learning (Tobin, Tippins, and Hook 1992). Constructivists agree that students individually construct a knowledge of science within a cultural setting with others. They have opportunities to compare knowledge, talk it over with peers, ask questions, justify their position, and arrive at a consensus. Learning is not merely the act of an individual, but a modified group interaction.

Science and math lessons may begin with real materials, invite interactive learning, and allow students to explore the various dimensions of thoughtfulness, subject matter, and real-world applications. The goal is to help learners construct a new set of expectations and establish a new state of understanding. When students make sense of something by connecting it to a set of personal, everyday experiences, constructivists call it *viable knowledge.* Good teachers strive to connect academic goals to practical problem solving and students' life experiences. Using such a real-world base embeds thinking skills into the curriculum, so that students are intensely involved in reasoning, elaborating, formulating hypotheses, and problem solving. Such inquiry-based learning cannot be isolated within calcified disciplinary boundaries.

Developing mature critical and creative thinkers who are able to acquire and use knowledge means educating minds rather than training memories. Sometimes the acquisition of enhanced thinking skills can be well-structured and planned, at other times it is a chance encounter formed by a crazy collision of elements. The ability to raise powerful interdisciplinary questions about what is being read, viewed, or heard is a dimension of thinking that makes a powerful contribution to the construction of meaning. When motivated to reason intelligently, children develop good decision-making and elaboration skills. Out of this comes insightful creations that suggest possibilities for action. As all of these elements come together, they form the core of effective thinking and learning.

The Dimensions of Thinking and Staff Development

Implementing new approaches to science and mathematics instruction depends on teachers who purposely invite reflective thinking. This means that both prospective and practicing teachers must take science and math courses in which they learn science through inquiry, and learn to apply mathematical concepts within a context similar to the one they will arrange for their students. When carried out over time, professional development activities have proven useful in helping teachers organize instruction to accommodate new ways of representing and imparting knowledge. The results expand horizons and organizational possibilities. When teachers *actually do* interdisciplinary inquiry they can reflect on teaching practices with colleagues and add to their ever-evolving base of good instructional practice.

Critical and creative thinking are natural human processes that can be developed with awareness and practice. Both critical and creative thinking make use of specific core thinking skills. Classroom instruction and guided practice in the development of these skills include the following:

1. Focusing skills—attending to selected chunks of information. Some focusing skills include defining, identifying key concepts, recognizing the problem, and setting goals.

2. Information-gathering skills—becoming aware of the substance or content needed. Observing, obtaining information, forming questions, and clarifying through inquiry are some skills of information gathering.

3. Remembering skills—using activities that involve information storage and retrieval. Encoding and recalling are thinking skills that have been found to improve retention. These skills involve strategies such as rehearsal, mnemonics, visualization, and retrieval.

4. Organizing skills—arranging information so that it can be understood or presented more effectively. Some of these organizing skills consist of comparing, classifying (categorizing), ordering, and representing information.

5. Analyzing skills—classifying and examining information about components and relationships. Analysis is at the heart of critical thinking. Recognizing and articulating attributes and component parts, focusing on details and structure, identifying relationships and patterns, grasping the main idea or thesis, and finding errors are elements of analysis.

6. Generating skills—using prior knowledge to add information beyond what is known or given. Connecting new ideas, inferring, identifying similarities and differences, predicting, and elaborating add new meaning to information. Generating in-

volves such higher order thinking as making comparisons, constructing metaphors, producing analogies, providing explanations, and forming mental models.

7. Integrating skills—putting things together, solving, understanding, forming principles, composing, and communicating. These thinking strategies involve summarizing, combining information, deleting unnecessary material, graphically organizing, outlining, and restructuring to incorporate new information.

8. Evaluating skills—assessing the reasonableness and quality of ideas. Skills of evaluation include establishing criteria and proving or verifying data (Marzano et al. 1988).

For teachers to build a solid base of thinking skills into daily science and math lessons requires that they consciously question and reflect on the best approach. Introspective questions about the characteristics of effective instruction help; for example, teachers must ask themselves: *How can I get students to focus their thinking, ask questions, retrieve new information, and generate new ideas for analysis?*

In addition to teaching about specific thinking skills, students need guidance in how to apply these skills to scientific and mathematical inquiry. Teachers must learn how to facilitate these skills by allowing opportunity for their use. As these skills are integrated into the curriculum and everyday classroom use, teachers should also ensure that

- students are given sufficient time to think before being required to answer questions

- interaction focuses on sustained examination of a few topics rather than superficial coverage of many

  students clarify or justify their opinions, rather than accept and reinforce them indiscriminately

- interactions are characterized by substantive coherence and continuity

- they model the characteristics of a thoughtful person (e.g., showing interest in students' ideas and their suggestions for solving problems, modeling problem-solving processes rather than just giving answers, and acknowledging the difficulties involved in gaining a clear understanding of problematic topics)

- students generate original and unconventional ideas in the course of the interaction (Newmann 1990, 1992)

Workshops on critical and scientific thinking often focus on four or five dimensions. The Association for Supervision and

Curriculum Development's (ASCD) Dimensions of Learning Program (DoLP), for example, focuses on positive learning attitudes toward thinking that lead to the acquisition and integration of knowledge. In this way, content is tied to the teaching of thinking. The Dimensions of Learning Program and other successful programs also work to develop the thinking involved in refining and extending knowledge, productive habits of the mind, and the thoughtful use of knowledge (ASCD 1994). Whatever labels are used, the steps shown here have proved popular and effective with science and math educators. This is partly because they are compatible with content, collaborative interaction, and what teachers are learning about mathematical reasoning, scientific processes, problem solving, and real-world applications.

Critical and Creative Thinking: Application and Self-Reliance

Beyond using manipulatives in math and discovery in science, teachers are bringing these subjects to life by setting thoughtful application problems in real-life contexts. Knowledge is particularly useful when it can be used to discover or create new knowledge. Students need opportunities to use their knowledge to compose, make decisions, solve problems, and conduct research to discover more. As teachers facilitate activities built on multiple ways of reasoning, doors are opened to the physical and biological universe.

The infusion of creative thinking into the science and math curriculum goes hand in hand with the basic principles students must learn to be competent in these subjects. Solid reasoning supports the foundation of interdisciplinary inquiry, real-world applications, and the production of new knowledge. In our efforts to bring science and math to life by making it relevant to students' daily lives, it is important to leave spaces where students and teachers can reflect on what they are doing and figure out where they will use the skills that they are learning. Critical and creative thinking has as much potential to impact government, business, the arts, and society as it does the sciences.

People who think creatively have the ability to produce and consider many alternatives by creating or elaborating on original ideas. Creative thinkers have the ability to see multiple solutions. Developing and expressing emotional awareness is a part of creative thinking. This is frequently done by perceiving and creating images that are vivid, strong, and alive both from an internal and external vantage point. Making use of imagination, movement, and sound in playful and useful ways is another element of creative thinking; likewise, so is overcoming limitations and creating new solutions, using humor, predicting consequences, and planning ahead. Students will learn elements of creative thinking from interpersonal communication behaviors. These are developed in a variety of ways: listening, speaking, arguing, problem solving, clarifying, and creating (Dissanayake 1992).

Thinking does not thrive in a threatening, intimidating environment where either adult or peer pressure impedes independence. Classrooms organized for creative science and math group work function as a community that respects individual learners. Good teachers support diverse thinking styles and collaboration, helping all students to think and step outside of subject matter and boundaries of experience to construct meaning.

The old view of teaching for the transmission of content has been expanded to include new intellectual tools and new ways of helping students thoughtfully construct knowledge on their own and with peers. Teachers who invite thoughtfulness understand that knowledge is to be shared or developed, rather than held by the authority. They arrange science and mathematics instruction so that students construct concepts, develop their thinking skills, and become more self-reliant. As a result, everyone involved becomes an active constructor of knowledge and more capable of making thoughtful decisions in the future.

Recognizing the development of thinking skills and self-reliance—in both the individual and the group—is an important first step toward application and assessment. Some possible guideposts for assessing development of self-reliant thinking and collaboration in students, and collectively in cooperative learning groups include

- decreasing the number of *How do I/we do it?* questions
- students asking group members before asking the teacher
- using trial-and-error discovery learning without frustration
- using metaphor, simile, and allegory in speaking, writing, and thinking
- developing interpersonal discussion skills for shared inquiry
- increasing their ability to work collaboratively in cooperative groups
- expanding their willingness to begin a task
- initiating inquiry

- increasing their comfort with ambiguity and open-ended assignments
- synthesizing and combining diverse ideas

It is hard to measure interpersonal, critical, and creative thinking skills and attitudes with a paper-and-pencil test. Observing the behavior, methodology, interaction, humor, anecdotes, and changes in individual and group behavior is often more effective and revealing. From these observations teachers become more informed decision makers themselves, as they monitor and modify the direction of the curriculum, supplementing as necessary. This ability—of both students and teachers—to pull together as a team, influences how well students reflect on their thinking and build self-reliance (Anderson and Burns 1989).

The Portfolio as an Assessment Tool

Portfolios represent the cutting edge of a more authentic and meaningful assessment process. They are a powerful performance assessment tool that requires students to select, collect, and reflect on what they are creating and accomplishing. Selecting the academic work that represents their thinking and interests provides another opportunity for students to use critical thinking skills. As students think about evidence that they have collected and decide what it means, they are participating in a meaningful critical and creative thinking experience.

Portfolios have long been associated with artists and photographers as a means of displaying collected samples of representative work. They have also been used for more than ten years in various reading and writing projects (Graves 1994). In the 1990s the National Assessment of Educational Progress suggested using portfolios to assess students' writing and reading abilities. In addition, portfolios have been helping whole language teachers monitor and evaluate student performance in the language arts for the better part of a decade. The interest in using these performance assessment techniques continues to expand the curriculum.

Although this performance assessment technique was slow in being adopted into the elementary science and mathematics curriculum, many teachers have found that the necessary collecting, organizing, and reflecting work that students need to do to prepare their portfolios complemented active, inquiry-based learning. It captures an authentic portrait of a child's thinking and can serve as an excellent conference tool for meetings with children, parents, and supervisors.

The Purpose and Design of a Portfolio

A portfolio can be described as a portrait of understanding; a device that contains physical evidence of someone's skills and dispositions. It is more than a folder full of a student's work: A portfolio represents a deliberate, specific collection of an individual's accomplishments. The items are carefully selected by the student and the teacher to represent a cross section of a student's critical and creative efforts.

Portfolios can be used as a vehicle to bring students together to discuss ideas and provide evidence of understanding and the ability to apply it. Likewise, the information accumulated in a portfolio assists teachers in determining learners' strengths and weaknesses; teachers can also use portfolios to help diagnose student learning difficulties. It is a tool that can be used to gain a more powerful understanding of student achievement, knowledge, attitudes, collaboration abilities, and the effectiveness of the curriculum. Portfolios are being used by math and science teachers to document students' development and focus on their growth over time. With the portfolio, the emphasis is on performance and application, rather than on knowledge for knowledge's sake.

The portfolio assessment process helps students become aware of their learning history and the development of their ability to reason in a scientific manner. As students become directly involved in the assessing process, the barrier between the learner and the assessment of the learner is lowered. Through critical analysis of their own work—and the work of peers—students gain insight into the many ways of thinking about and resolving a problem. As they develop new understandings of their own thinking they become more accomplished in evaluating their own work.

Building a portrait of a student's understanding is not a one-time collection of examples. Portfolios are a means of bringing together representative material created over time. This material should reflect students' knowledge and performance. The purpose is to gain an accurate understanding of students' work, development, and growth. The intent is to document the past to shape the future more effectively. Therefore, when determining the scope and design of a particular portfolio, careful attention should be given to

- what is being assessed
- the design of the portfolio
- the appropriateness of the contents to what is being assessed
- the audience for which it is intended

The purpose behind the portfolio should determine its design. The range and the depth can be determined by the teacher, the student, or the nature of the portfolio's contents. Students may choose the contents based on specific categories. For example, teachers could ask students to select samples of their work that fit into categories such as

- a problem that was difficult
- where understanding of a problem began
- a solution to a problem
- a new understanding of a problem
- a problem that required new ideas to solve
- two items of which the student is proud
- one example of a comical disaster

Involving students in the selection process gets them directly participating in their own learning and their own evaluation, thus promoting intellectual autonomy and self-respect. Learners, teachers, and parents can gain a better understanding of the student in and out of school because portfolio contents can reveal a surprising depth of thinking and provide insight into personal issues. Collecting, organizing, and reflecting on their school experience and that of their peers allow students to communicate who they are and how they view themselves in relation to others. Portfolios may include such things as

- group assignments and team ideas
- teacher comments and assessments
- student writings and experimental designs
- student reflections, journal entries, reactions, and feelings
- collected data entries, logs, and research
- problems and investigations
- individual and group projects
- creative expressions, art, audio- and videotapes, and photographs
- rough drafts and polished products (Mumme 1990)

Items selected should be dated and accompanied by a caption or description of the item. A cover letter by the student, a table of contents, and a description of the assignment or task are ways of developing a sense of organizational skills and pride in the student, while also assisting the reader. As the portfolio develops, the contents can be added to, deleted, improved, revised, edited, or discarded. Each element can represent a different form of expression and means of representing the knowledge and skills acquired.

Practical Questions Frequently Asked About Portfolios

What type of physical container would hold representative pieces?
For older students a three-ring binder is most frequently used for items such as oral history interviews, copies of historical documents, photos of community service activities, worksheets, and class notes. Handouts can be three-hole punched and added, along with journal entries, written comments, quizzes, and other documents. Students may wish to purchase three-ring separators with folder compartments to stick in maps, magazines, software disks, and so forth. More elaborate kinds of three-ring notebook containers include plastic casings in which pictures, articles, posters, and so on, can be added.

An artist's folder (portfolio container) is useful for gathering things like video cassettes and three-dimensional kinds of projects. The cardboard folder has a string closure to prevent things from falling out. They are fairly inexpensive and come in a variety of sizes— from 3 × 5 in. for index cards, to 3 × 3 ft. for larger projects. For the sake of representation in the portfolio, photographs can be taken of large projects and videotapes made of others.

Elementary teachers often use large boxes. Students place their written work in folders by subject area and the folder is put in a decorated box with the student's name. Other kinds of items are also included in the box (copies of artifacts, relief maps, and so on). The items may change month by month, but the boxes are kept for the year. Selected treasures remain. Boxes are stacked for easy access and neatness.

A combination of containers may be the best approach, depending on the contents and nature of the assessment.

Who uses portfolios?
Portfolio assessment is not just for younger students. Portfolios can be used for students from kindergarten through graduate school.

How are portfolios evaluated?
This is a partial list of some suggested criteria for evaluating student portfolios:

1. Evidence of critical and creative thinking—Does the student's work show that he or she has

   - demonstrated an understanding of the responsibilities of citizenship?

   - organized and displayed information that goes beyond statistical data?

   - included other items on which the student worked in the problem/project?

   - conjectured, explored, analyzed, looked for patterns, and so forth?

   - used the intellectual tools of analog and inquiry?

   - evidenced an understanding of democratic values and social responsibility?

   - used concrete materials and/or drawings or sketches as an aid in interpreting and analyzing problems/issues?

   - used technology, such as video excerpts, computers, graphics, or calculators, as a tool in suggesting possible solutions to problems?

   - searched out, explored, critically examined, and included research data?

2. Quality of activities and investigations—Do the student's activities or investigations help him or her develop an understanding of significant concepts? Do the activities cut across several areas of math and science inquiry?

3. Variety of approaches and investigations—Does the portfolio provide evidence that the student used a variety of approaches? Does the portfolio include a variety of resources and provide research to support opinions and different approaches to solving a problem? Does the portfolio include different activities or investigations?

4. Understanding and skill in situations that parallel prior classroom experience—Does the portfolio provide evidence that the student knows why he or she is using certain procedures or a particular approach, or what the data mean?

The portfolio assessment should be integrative and oriented toward critical thinking and solving problems, not simply recall based. Some other integrative assessments that can be added to the portfolio include observational notes by the teacher, student self-assessment, and progress notes written by the teacher and student (often written collaboratively).

Activities Using Critical and Creative Inquiry Skills

Activity Title: Sound Mapping

Purpose and Objectives
By mapping sound in an outdoor environment, students will use the inquiry skills of observing, recording, and communicating. This activity allows students to experiment with different ways that sounds can be described. After ten minutes of listening and drawing students will be able to describe and show what they have heard and where they heard it by looking at their personal maps.

Materials

- one or more compasses
- paper and pencils for each student
- a clipboard or other hard surface on which to write for each student

Procedure
Ask students to name the five senses, then tell them that they are going to be using the sense of hearing to create a sound map. Pass out paper to students and have them draw four equal boxes on the paper. Have students mark each of the ends of their lines with North on the top, South on the bottom, West on the left, and East on the right. Find an open area where you can space students at least ten feet apart. Next, using a compass, find due north and have students face in that direction. Tell the students that for the next five to ten minutes they should draw what they hear in the area on their paper where they hear it. During the time they are drawing they should not talk. When time is up have the students form a circle and share their maps, as well as point out one or two sounds they heard and how they noted it on their map.

Evaluation, Completion, and/or Follow-up
The drawing of sound and the ensuing discussion afterward enables students to better understand the different sources of sounds and how to describe what they hear to other people in a variety of ways.

Activity Title: To Observe and Describe Using the Five Senses

Purpose and Objectives
This K–2 primary activity uses the five senses. The process skills of observing, inferring, communicating, sharing, and hypothesizing are

introduced. Children will observe and make inferences with their senses. They will talk and share their ideas with others, ask questions, and make hypotheses based on their senses. Children will verify their thinking through personal experiences.

Materials

- several "safe" objects (see procedure)
- paper bags

Procedure

Select several objects that are safe to touch, smell, and taste (cookie, orange, apple, and popcorn are good choices). Put each object in a clean paper bag and ask students to feel the object without looking inside. Have the children describe what they feel. Have the children smell the object without peeking. Encourage students to describe what they smell. Shake the bag and invite students to describe what they hear. Next, you may wish to have the students taste the object and describe it. Finally, allow students to look at the object and verify their guesses.

Evaluation, Completion, and/or Follow-up

It is important to discuss with students the strategies they used in making their guesses. Point out the invaluable role of others. Ask what they learned from other classmates about making inferences. Experiences such as these in inferring and describing give children an opportunity to develop and refine many scientific and mathematical concepts. Children may use vague or emotional terms rather than specific descriptive words. It is important to discuss the communication process and which words are most effective in describing what they did. Let children discuss which words give better descriptions. Have children relate their everyday language to scientific and mathematical language and symbols.

Activity Title: Exploring Structures

Purpose and Objectives

There are many kinds of structures that can be described in the natural world. This beginning activity attempts to show how different kinds of structures are related. In this activity children will find out about supports. The skills introduced include experimenting, testing strength and durability, comparing size and weight, recording data, and communicating. Children will discover these skills by building a tower. This activity is designed so that when presented with a problem of how to support their tower, students will explore solutions by working with materials. Children will discuss and share their discoveries with other class members after experimenting and trying many different support structures. Children will compare their tower supports with other children. Students will test the strength of their tower.

Materials

- items to form a tower: a cardboard box, a tall block of wood, a paper towel roll
- support materials: styrofoam, wood, cartons, cardboard boxes, and so on
- clay, sand, and white glue
- art materials: paints, brushes, construction paper, scissors, paste, and felt-tip pens

Procedure

Introduce the activity by talking about structures, the classroom, tables in the room, and so on. Generate questions, such as: *What makes the ceiling stay where it is? What keeps the table from falling?* Children will soon come up with the idea of structural support. Discuss these ideas with the class. Explain that the name we give to these items is structural support. Explain to the students that they are to build a tower. Challenge the students to find a way to make their tower stand up so that it cannot be blown over in a strong wind. Provide them with some helpful ideas for getting started, such as gluing supports around the base of the tower, filling a box with sand, attaching the base to a larger surface, and setting the tower in sand or clay.

After children have determined a way to support their towers, have them share what they found out. Have the children compare their solutions and test their towers to see how strong they are. For example, children may decide to test their tower by having five or six students blow on it at the same time, or they could place a fan near their tower and turn it on to see if the tower stands up. Encourage students to experiment further with different supports to make their towers as sturdy as they can be. Have children decorate their towers with the art supplies provided.

Evaluation, Completion, and/or Follow-up

To find out how much the students learned about supports, present them with another challenge: Can they build a balcony using the materials they have? Students can test it by adding weights. How many weights (if any) will each balcony hold? Add more and more weights until it begins to show signs of collapsing. (This activity was adapted from *Constructions*, by Joan Westley [1988]).

Activity Title: Magnets and Attraction

Purpose and Objectives

Given a group of materials and a magnet, groups of students will predict and then test whether or not the objects are attracted to the magnet. Students will record their findings in their journal and hypothesize (or guess) why some objects are attracted while others are not, while developing the process skills of describing, predicting, experimenting, forming hypotheses, testing predictions, recording data, inferring, and recognizing cause-and-effect relationships. Students will review and discuss their findings with the class (sharing their discoveries and comparing them with other groups), and actively participate in their groups. Each student will learn that magnets only attract certain metal objects—iron and steel.

Materials

- sacks or brown bags (to hold objects to test)
- magnets (large enough for students to handle with ease)
- paper, notebooks or science/math journal
- approximately 20 objects (about half of which should be attracted to the magnet), such as: tacks, nails, rubber bands, pieces of sponge, paper clips, pins, pebbles, chalk, needles, coins, wood, paper, pencils, copper, glass, plastic, screws, aluminum, cloth, and leather

Procedure

Divide students into groups of four to six. Present this problem to the class: Which of these objects are magnetic? Assign jobs, or have students determine jobs themselves, such as material handler, record keeper, object displayer (from the bag), and clean-up. Before letting students get their supplies, explain to them that each group will be given a magnet and a bag of objects. Have the students view their objects one at a time, make a prediction as to whether or not it will be attracted to the magnet, and then test the object. Instruct the students to record both predictions and results in their notebook. After the objects have been tested, have the students review and discuss their findings, and answer these questions: *What do the objects that were attracted to the magnet have in common? What do the objects that were not attracted have in common? What can you conclude from your investigation?*

Then have groups of students see how many objects they can find in the classroom that are attracted to their magnet. Have the students keep a list of all the things that are attracted to their group's magnet.

Ask the students to share their group's findings with the class. Encourage them to compare and discuss what other groups found out.

Evaluation, Completion, and/or Follow-up
Group written work along with oral discussion provides feedback as to whether or not students are understanding the concept of magnetism. Direct students to write what they learned about magnetism. Have them reflect on their group's process, expressing their knowledge as well as their impressions about magnetism.

Activity Title: Recyclable Materials Construction: Hands-on Technology

Purpose and Objectives
This activity moves beyond conducting experiments or finding solutions to word problems. In hands-on technology, students are not shown a solution. This will allow students to supply many creative designs. During the course of solving their problem, students will be forced to test scientific hypotheses and frequently generate new questions (Hamm 1992). This activity will involve scientific investigation and mathematical problem solving, but it is quite different from routine classroom tasks. In this activity, a problem will be introduced to the class. Working in small groups of four or five students, the students will be challenged to plan a way of coming up with a solution. Students will document the steps they used along the way, brainstorm, discuss the problem with the group, draw pictures, show design ideas, use mathematics, present technical drawings, work together, and consult with other students who have already solved the problems.

Materials
- plastic milk jugs and soda bottles
- aluminum cans
- newspaper
- wood
- electrical supplies
- glue
- tape

The emphasis here is on using recyclable materials, so many supplies can be obtained from the students.

Procedure

Divide the students into groups of four or five. Challenge them to de-sign and construct the lightest and strongest beam possible with one or more recyclable materials (e.g., aluminum cans, plastic milk jugs, plastic soda bottles, newspaper). Establish a common beam length for all groups (usually four or five feet). Have the students gather informa-tion from a variety of resources and sketch all the possibilities they considered and record the scientific, mathematical, and technological principles used. Before the students begin testing their beam, have them work together to organize the testing procedures. Have each group determine a common unit of weight for testing the beams and increasing the load. Have the students weigh the beam. Then test it by supporting it at each end and applying a load to the middle. Have them increase the load until the beam breaks. Inform the students that the load divided by the beam weight will gives the load-to-weight ratio.

Evaluation, Completion, and/or Follow-up

Have the students document their work in a portfolio that includes

- sketches of all the possibilities their group considered
- a graphic showing how their invention performed
- descriptions of the scientifc, mathematical, and technological prin-ciples used in their solution
- information and notes gathered from resources
- thoughts and reflections about this project

(This activity was adapted from Mark Sanders [1994], TSM Inte-gration Program, *School Science and Mathematics*.)

Chapter Three

Teaching Science: Engaging Students in Scientific Inquiry

Some important themes pervade science, mathematics, and technology, and appear over and over again, whether we are looking at an ancient civilization, the human body, or a comet. They are ideas that transcend disciplinary boundaries and prove fruitful in explanation, in theory, and in design.
—Rutherford and Ahlgren, *Science for All Americans*

Science is a system of knowing about the universe—large and small, near and far. This knowledge is acquired through information gathered by observation and experimentation, and the development of sound inquiry process skills. One important goal of science instruction is to expand students' perception and appreciation of the very nature of life—water, rocks, plants, animals, people, and other elements of the world around us and beyond. Through this understanding students develop a spate of protean learning and reasoning skills. These skills transfer easily across the disciplines of mathematics and technology, and allow students to use their acquired knowledge in a versatile, productive way, while also building self-reliance and confidence.

Science education and curriculum, like the very nature of science itself, is constantly changing. As the tools and methods of discovery improve, so does understanding—although not without the caveat that error is an organic part of the process. In scientific inquiry, mistakes are simply steps toward more complete comprehension. Scientific discovery has spawned technology; technology feeds on scientific discovery and requires copious amounts for sustenance. Today's science classroom must prepare students to exist within the demands of this paradox. National standards have been created to establish common goals and chart a course for districts and schools to follow; however, if learning is accomplished in the trenches, then it is the teacher and the curriculum that directly affects the students and the development of their scientific inquiry process skills. Conceptual themes that span all areas of scientific thinking form the foundation of today's science curriculum. Integrating these themes is a significant challenge faced by educators.

Changes in Science Education

In spite of the early efforts of Dewey and others, the science curriculum focused on content until the late 1950s. In 1957 the Soviet Union sent up the first orbiting space satellite, Sputnik. This event prompted a national call for higher educational standards, and changes in science education were seen as "vital to national security" (Tolman and Hardy 1995). Science educators in the United States began to shift their emphasis away from content and toward process. (Process is how a scientist or mathematician thinks, works, and studies problems.) The science inquiry (process) approach began to take shape and definition in the 1960s, and resulted in the structure of science education as we know it today. Although revised and improved, this carefully studied method proved itself and is more vital today than ever.

The process approach was embellished in the 1970s with the added idea of a unified science education (combining the various sciences), and in the 1980s with the introduction of the science/technology/society components of the science curriculum. In the 1990s the national standards for science education were constructed on these foundations.

An Overview of the National Science Education Standards

In the mid 1990s, the demand for modern, comprehensive science education standards began to be filled. The National Academy Press (National Academy of Sciences 1996) published the *National Science Education Standards* report at the end of 1995; by the spring of 1996 it had been distributed to school districts across the country. The NSTA published related material: Their *Pathways to the Science Standards* is a set of three practical guidebooks for helping teachers at all grade levels put the standards into practice. Both the standards and the guidebooks can be ordered by calling 800-722-NSTA.

The principles that guide the National Science Education Standards are paraphrased as follows:

1. Science is for all students.
2. Learning is an active process.
3. School science reflects the intellectual and cultural traditions that characterize the practice of contemporary science.
4. Improving science education is part of systemic educational reform.

The content standards highlight what students should know, understand, and be able to do. The standards, paraphrased as follows, indicate that students should be able to

- connect the concepts and processes in science
- use science as inquiry
- become aware of physical, life, earth, and space science through activity-based learning
- use science understandings to design solutions to problems
- understand the relationship of science and technology
- view and practice science in personal and social perspectives
- identify with the history and nature of science through readings, discussions, observations, and written communications

Although content standards are crucial, successful reform of science education requires addressing issues like the instructional support system, teacher education, assessment, and the school culture. The science standards are comprehensive, and go beyond *content* and *performance* areas found in the math standards to address professional development standards, assessment standards, system standards, and so on. The National Science Education Standards, as paraphrased, call for the following:

- the consistency of the science program with other standards and across grade levels
- the coordination of the science program with mathematics education
- the provision of appropriate and sufficient resources for all students
- the provision of equitable opportunities for all students
- the opportunity to learn about the topics suggested in the standards
- the development of communities that encourage, support, and sustain teachers

The program standards also call for the inclusion of all content standards in a variety of curricula that are appropriate, interesting, relevant to student's lives, organized around inquiry, and connected to other school subjects.

Science Education Today

When taught as an active, hands-on subject, science can be an exciting experience for both students and teachers. By connecting with other disciplines, science can also provide imaginative teachers with many opportunities for integration with other subjects, such as mathematics. To use and understand science today requires an awareness of how scientific endeavors embrace other related domains—like math and technology—and how they relate to our culture and our lives.

Effective science teachers are usually those who have built up their science knowledge base and developed a repertoire of current pedagogical techniques. Many skilled science teachers now begin by making connections between science, mathematics, technology, and real-world concerns of the type that might be found in a good newspaper. By stressing real investigations and participatory learning, these teachers move children from the concrete to the abstract, as they explore the major conceptual themes that run through science, mathematics, and technology.

Teaching strategies in elementary and middle school science now include participatory experiences and opportunities for students to explore science in their lives. The emphasis is on thinking skills, work teams, cooperative learning, and inquiry. This approach requires students to pose questions, make observations, read, plan investigations, experiment, propose explanations, and communicate the results. By developing effective interpersonal skills, students can work together to frame questions and to examine data critically. This growth is supplemented by designing and conducting real experiments that carry their thinking beyond the classroom. As science and mathematics instruction becomes more connected to children's lives, enriching questions and insights arise from inquiring about their real-world concerns.

Most science educators today agree that science can best be viewed as a continuous process of trying to discover order in nature and looking for consistent patterns of the universe through systematic study. The *question* is the cornerstone of investigation: It guides the inquirer to a variety of sources, revealing previously undetected patterns. These openings into understanding can become sources of new questions that can deepen and enhance inquiry. Science becomes thinking and asking questions about the workings of the universe. The scientific method (process) becomes an intellectual tool that is as important as the tools of analog for History or metaphor for English.

The Thematic Teaching of Science

Themes are often called the big ideas, or the building blocks, of a discipline. Themes provide a unifying structure that is helpful in guiding teachers as they develop instructional tools. They can be used to integrate concepts and facts throughout all areas of the curriculum. Some science educators are concerned that thematic scientific inquiry means that the usual curricular divisions of earth, life, and physical science may be diminished. Just the opposite is true: As disciplines rapidly expand, a thematic approach serves as a powerful way of uniting or transferring knowledge from one field to the next. If these connections are successful, then it is hoped these intellectual habits will carry over and enrich other fields and disciplines. As a result, students may start to see more clearly the overall purpose and logic of the educational system. Thus an integrative approach to inquiry will not only help them develop a meaningful structure for understanding science, but also see the relationship to other subjects and their daily lives.

There are several criteria developed by Martinello and Cook (1994) to help teachers decide if a theme is important and meaningful. The criteria are paraphrased as follows:

1. Is the big idea constant over space and time?
2. Does it broaden students' understanding of the world or what it means to be human?
3. Is the big idea interdisciplinary?
4. Does the theme relate to the genuine interests of students?
5. Does the interdisciplinary work lend itself to student inquiry?

In the inquiry-based science classroom, themes can provide elements of cohesion that allow students to develop a basis for comparison, contrast, and Boolean patterns. A sampling of scientific themes from Rutherford and Algren (1990), paraphrased as follows, includes

- systems and interactions—a collection of things that can have some influence on one another and appear to constitute a unified whole (e.g., the number system, educational system, solar system, weather system, oxygen system, monetary system, systems of time, measurement system, garbage system, telephone system, electric system, sound system, communication system)
- models—a simple representation that can help others understand it better (e.g., a pump is a model used to represent a heart)
- constancy—ways in which systems do not change; a state of equilibrium.
- patterns of change—patterns that are used to understand what will happen and to predict what will happen
- evolution—the present arose from the forms of the past; all natural things and systems change through time
- scale and structure—the minute and immense magnitudes in the universe (e.g., size, duration, speed) which are closely tied to systems, because most systems are studied at some scale
- energy—a central concept of the physical sciences that pervades mathematical, biological, and geological sciences because it underlies any system of interactions: in physical terms—the capacity to do work or the ability to make things move; in chemical terms—the basis for reactions between compounds; in biological terms—the basis for living systems to maintain their systems, to grow, and to reproduce

Inquiry Process Skills

Students need to be exposed to a basic body of knowledge, attitudes, and skills that will build a foundation for future discoveries. Being able to use the knowledge and skills of science, mathematics, and technology in a meaningful way may be the most important objective for students in their learning process. Meaningful learning implies active student control over the content learned, as well as being able to use the knowledge practically in a personal way. Manipulating and adapting ideas, learning through experience, creating knowledge, and enhancing appreciation for the laws and principles that guide learners are part of the inquiry process.

Science and math teachers should strive to include each of these skills in their curriculum. The process skills must be supported to ensure that lessons are built on the curiousity of children as well as on curricular content (Frederick and Cheesebrough 1993). As learners *construct* knowledge (or process, as Piaget explains it) rather than accumulate it, they make science, mathematics, and technology relevant and personal. Teachers should introduce and plan class inquiry discussions and activities that cover each skill.

Observing

Observing involves using all of the senses: seeing, hearing, tasting, smelling, and feeling. Effective observation uses all the primary senses, working together to gather as much information as possible. It is an immediate reaction to one's environment. Students should be directed to describe what they see, hear, smell, touch, and perhaps taste. Teachers should train and encourage students to give some specific measurements to their observations. Teachers should caution students not to influence their observations by adding the teacher's interpretations. Even young children should be able to make significant observations. Observation is the foundation for all other inquiry process skills. Observations are the uninterpreted facts of science and mathematics.

Classifying

Classifying relies primarily on observation. As students become more skilled in recognizing characteristics of objects, they learn to recognize likenesses and differences. Classification is an important part of our lives: Shopping at the supermarket, finding a book in the library, or even setting the dinner table would be a tremendous, time-consuming chore if things weren't classified. At a young age children are able to classify, or sort, objects into groups by color, size, or shape; rearrange the set; and put the groups in some kind of order.

Comparing

Once children learn to observe and describe objects, they soon begin to compare them. Young children may say they want more or fewer, and they can tell what is the same or different. Being able to compare individual and sets of objects will help children decide whether four is more or less than six. Comparing is not just a skill for students in the early grades: Students will use this skill in every grade and throughout their work in every discipline.

Sequencing

Students live with sequences and patterns. They may notice patterns in nature, such as the symmetry of a leaf and the wings of an insect. They can observe patterns in buildings, such as the way bricks fit together or the markings on the floor. Sequencing is finding or bringing order to their observations. The patterns that exist all around students are enlivened when teachers direct student observation and pattern-finding activities.

Measuring

Active experiences in science provide many opportunities to describe and compare in terms of quantity. Young children automatically use numbers when comparing quantities—one child is taller than another, one book is heavier, one ball is larger, and so forth. Measuring supplies the hard data necessary to confirm hypotheses and make predictions. It provides first-hand, quantifiable information. Measuring includes gathering data on size, weight, and quantity. Measurement tools (e.g., rulers, thermometers, scales) and skills have a variety of uses in everyday life. Being able to measure connects science and mathematics to the environment.

Communicating

Communication skills stress the importance of being able to talk, write, describe, and explain science and mathematical ideas. Symbolism, along with visual aids such as charts and graphs, will become part of the ways students can express their scientific and mathematical ideas to others. This means that students should learn not only to interpret the language of science and mathematics, but to use that language both in and beyond the classroom. All students will expand their knowledge base and increase their learning abilities by regularly talking, writing, drawing, and graphing; and using symbols, numbers, and tables to help them think and communicate their ideas. By making sense to others, they indirectly convey the concept in a meaningful way for themselves.

The language of science and mathematics is interrelated, as are scientific and mathematical thinking. Likewise, these processes are interrelated to students' everyday lives. They overlap and reinforce one another. If students practice thinking and communicating scientifically and mathematically, and connect their skills to their everyday experiences, they will discover a wealth of new techniques in both areas.

Learning to communicate effectively makes the world of science and mathematics outside of school more accessible. It also promotes interaction and the investigation of ideas within the classroom, as students learn in an active, verbal environment. Working with science and mathematics to communicate benefits all students, as they experience the precision of speech and writing that good science and mathematics demands.

Using Data

The disciplines of science and mathematics identify statistics and probability as important links to many content areas. The skills of data gathering, analyzing, recording, using tables, and reading graphs provide many opportunities for representing, interpreting, and recording that applies many scientific and mathematical concepts and skills.

Many decisions are based on research and projections. If these data are to be understood and used, students must be able to process such information efficiently. For example, consider the scientific and mathematical concepts involved in the following:

- weather reports—decimals, percentages, probability, weather patterns, climate zones, weather fronts, temperatures, humidity readings, etc.
- public opinion polls—sampling techniques, errors of measurement, numbers of participants, breakdowns of result, and so on
- advertising claims—hypothesis testing, product research, polls, sales records, projections, and so on
- monthly government reports—unemployment, inflation, interest rates, energy supplies, budget analysis, and so on

All media depend on these techniques for summarizing information. Radio, television, and newspapers bombard us with statistical information. The current demand for information-processing skills continues to grow as students live and learn in a statistically charged context.

Graphing

Graphing skills include constructing and reading graphs, and interpreting graphic information. These skills should be introduced in early grades. The data should depend on children's interest and maturity. Here are a few kinds of survey data that could be collected in the classroom:

- physical characteristics—height, eye color, shoe size
- sociological characteristics—birthday, number of family members, number of pets
- personal preferences—favorite television show, favorite book, favorite sport, favorite food

Each of these concepts gives students the opportunity to collect data themselves.

Graphs are an important form of communication in science and mathematics. Graphic messages can provide large amounts of information at a glance. Graphs are often used to make predictions. In creating a graph it is important to make the graph large and clear enough for the students to manipulate, and for the other students to make interpretations, predictions, or analyses (Heddens and Speer 1994).

Using Language

Language is a window into students' thinking and understanding. For most individuals, oral language is the primary means of communication. One of the overriding objectives in the cooperative learning classroom is to facilitate the use of oral language and listening as a means of communication and learning. Language also reveals the quality of the students' scientific and mathematical communication. Listening to students' language is a valuable way to get feedback from students' efforts. There are many ways to give students opportunities to practice and use language effectively. Effective communication will, of course, depend on topical knowledge, but also on students being aware of how to go about communicating orally.

Sharing

The process of sharing helps students feel more comfortable and less inhibited in speaking before an audience. Students develop independence as they share their work and ideas (Templeton 1991). Class discussions are held after the children have had time to explore a particular activity or idea. Teachers use these group sharing times to summarize and interpret data from explorations. Group sharing is a time for students to discuss their ideas, focus on scientific and mathematical relationships, and make connections among activities.

Using Space-Time Relationships

As children compare, classify, and sequence objects, they soon look at relationships among objects. Relationships are rules or agreements used to associate one or more objects or concepts with another. Science and mathematics is a collection of relationships among objects or concepts. A basic relationship in nature is the connection between air, food, water, and space. This variety of factors affects the ability of wildlife to maintain their survival over time. Everything in natural systems is interrelated. If one of these needs was eliminated the animal population would dwindle and die. In mathematics there are also many examples of relationships. Ideas such as six, triangle, ones/tens/hundreds (as in place value), sum, product, ratio, and equivalent are all examples of relationships.

Predicting

Children learn that not all predictions are accurate. Often there is a high degree of uncertainty in predicting. The ability to make predictions is based on skillful observation, inference, quantification, and communication. Students who understand predicting are aware that unforeseen events can change the conditions of a prediction and that one hundred percent accuracy is not likely.

Estimating

The curriculum should include estimation so students can develop estimation strategies, which will allow them to recognize when an estimation is appropriate, determine the reasonableness of results, and apply estimation in working with quantities, measurement, computation, and problem solving (NCTM Standards).

Inferring

The basic process skill of inference involves making conclusions based on reasoning. Inferences are based on observations and experiences. Students are often very creative in making inferences based on what they have observed. Inferences extend observation by allowing learners to explain their findings and predict what they think will happen.

The basic inquiry processes just discussed are global in their application, and not limited to scientific and mathematical investigation. For example, students might use the process of inference to try to understand why their teacher was angry with them in the lab yesterday. A student might sort and classify her supplies for a field trip.

Multiple Intelligences

To make learning accessible to the greatest number of students, teachers must have a functional awareness of different learning styles and multiple ways of making meaning. The brain has a multiplicity of functions and voices that speak independently and distinctly for different individuals. Howard Gardner's framework for multiple entry points to knowledge has had a powerful influence on the science and math standards (Gardner 1983, 1993). The standards clearly recognize alternative paths to learning and provide a framework for thinking about science and mathematics that is built on recognizing the uniqueness of each child, paraphrased as follows:

- verbal-linguistic—the ability to use language to excite, convince, and convey information
- logical-mathematical—the ability to explore patterns and relationships by manipulating objects or symbols in an orderly manner
- musical-rhythmic—the ability to perform, compose, or enjoy a musical piece
- spatial-visual—the ability to understand and mentally manipulate a form or object in a visual or spatial display
- body-kinesthetic—the ability to use motor skills in sports, performing arts, or art productions
- interpersonal—the ability to get along with others
- intrapersonal—the ability to understand one's inner feelings, dreams, and ideas

It is possible to take issue with Gardner on several points, such as not fully addressing spiritual and artistic modes of thought; however, there is general agreement on the central theme of his theory, which is the understanding that *intelligence is not a single capacity that every human being possesses to a greater or lesser extent.* There are multiple ways of knowing and learning. Consequently the methods of instruction should reflect different ways of knowing. For example, basing a lesson about birds on Gardner's theory of multiple intelligences might include the following:

- spatial—exploring maps of bird's migration patterns, photographs of birds, and artwork by students
- musical—listening to tapes of live bird sounds and imitating them, creating a rhythm or rap to accompany the tape
- kinesthetic—hiking to a bird's habitat and constructing a replica of a bird's nest
- intrapersonal—finding a quiet place of solitude for bird watching
- interpersonal—working with a local community or group conservation project to protect local bird habitat
- linguistic—writing stories or poems, or preparing book reports, oral presentations, and video- or audiotape recordings
- logical-mathematical—collecting statistics about birds and exploring work done by scientists about bird flight (migration patterns, how birds fly)

Do these seven *intelligences* adequately address all learning styles? Productive theories, like the one just presented, are more precise and therefore take on the risk of being proved off the mark. But unlike the usual vague psychological theory, this one has direct implications for teaching. And working out the ecology of thoughtfulness requires taking a risk with bolder and more explicit insights.

Scientific Inquiry Activities

Activity Title:
Exploring Water Cohesion and Surface Tension

Purpose and Objectives
Students will attempt to determine how many drops of water will fit on a penny in an experiment that demonstrates water cohesion and surface tension.

Materials

- one penny for each pair of students
- glasses of water
- paper towels
- eye droppers (one for each pair of students)

Procedure
Have students work with a partner. As a class, have them guess how many drops of water will fit on a penny. Record the guesses on the chalkboard. Ask students if it would make a difference if the penny was heads or tails. Record these guesses on the chalkboard also. Instruct the students to try the experiment by using an eye dropper, a penny, and a glass of water. Encourage students to record their findings in their science and math journal. Bring the class together again. Encourage students to share their findings with the class. On the chalkboard record their responses. Introduce the concept of cohesion. (Cohesion is the attraction of like molecules for each other. In solids the force is strongest. It is cohesion that holds a solid together. There is also an attraction among water molecules for each other.) Introduce and discuss the idea of surface tension. (The molecules of water on the surface hold together so well that they often keep heavier objects from breaking through. The surface acts as if it is covered with skin.)

Evaluation, Completion, and/or Follow-up
Have students explain how this activity showed surface tension. Instruct students to draw what surface tension looked like in their science and math journal. What makes the water drop break on the surface of the penny? (It is gravity.) What other examples can students think of where water cohesion can be observed? (Rain on a car windshield or window in a classroom, for example.)

Activity Title: Water Pressure Experiment—What Will Float?

Purpose and Objectives
Through this activity, primary students will discover the effects of gravity and water pressure in a series of observations of items that will or will not float.

Materials

- large plastic bowl
- salt
- bag of small objects to test (e.g., paper clip, nail, block, key)
- ruler
- spoon
- oil-base modeling clay
- paper towels
- large washers
- kitchen foil cut into six-inch squares

Explain to the students that the weight of water gives it pressure. For an object to float, opposing balanced forces work against each other. Gravity pulls down on the object, and the water pushes it up. If an object has a high volume and is light for its size, then it has a large surface area against which the water will push. Likewise, adding salt to the water will increase its density and make it more buoyant.

Procedure
Have the students fold the foil so there is one inch on all four sides of the tinfoil boat. There should be enough room to place the objects inside. Have the students fill the plastic bowls half full with water. Direct the students to empty the bag of objects onto the table. Next, have students separate the objects into two groups: objects that will float and objects that will sink. Encourage students to record their predictions in their science and math journal. Have students experiment by trying to float all the objects and record what happens in their science and math journal. Then, have the students add salt to the water, and repeat their experiments.

Evaluation, Completion, and/or Follow-up
Encourage students to reflect on these questions and respond in their science and math journal:

1. What is similar about all the objects that floated? sank?
2. What can be done to sink the objects that floated?
3. What can be done to float the objects that sank?
4. In what ways can a piece of foil be made to float? sink?
5. Describe how a foil boat can be made.
6. How many washers will the foil boat carry?
7. What can float in saltwater that cannot float in freshwater?
8. Encourage students to try to find something that will float in freshwater and sink in salt water.

(This activity was adapted from *Science In Elementary Education*, [Gega 1994]).

Activity Title: Observe the Presence of Air in the Soil

Purpose and Objectives
Through this activity, primary students will observe the presence of air in soil and other materials by conducting experiments that displace, or force, the available air out of the material.

Materials
- tumbler
- water
- soil

Procedure
Have students put some loose soil in a tumbler until it is half full. Next, have students pour water into the tumbler until the tumbler is almost full. Instruct students to observe the soil and record what happens in their science and math journal. (Bubbles of air will escape from the soil, indicating the presence of air in the soil.)

Evaluation, Completion, and/or Follow-up
Encourage students to write in their journal what they found out by doing this experiment. To pursue this further, ask students to investigate what articles contain air, such as crackers, stones, pieces of brick, coins, orange peels, leather, and so forth. Have students respond in their journal to the results of their experiments. Encourage students to infer which objects are likely to contain air by observing their physical properties. Describe the properties of objects that contain or do not

contain air. Have students devise a generalization concerning how they can find out what things contain air.

Activity Title: Observe That Air Occupies Space

Purpose and Objectives
Through this experiment, students will observe that although air—a gas—is invisible, it does take up space and have volume.

Materials

- paper towel
- tumbler
- aquarium
- water

Procedure
Instruct students to crumple a dry paper towel and stuff it into a tumbler so that it will not fall out when the tumbler is held upside down. Next, while holding the tumbler upside down, have students push the tumbler straight down to the bottom of an aquarium or large glass jar that is filled with water. Direct students to observe that the water does not fill the tumbler. Ask students to explain why this is so. (The space in the tumbler is occupied by air.) Have students tilt the tumbler slightly and ensure students see the air as it escapes from the tumbler in the form of bubbles. Now have students lift the tumbler straight out of the water and remove the paper towel. Have students note that it is still dry.

Evaluation, Completion, and/or Follow-up
Have students write their remarks about this experiment in their science and math journal. Ask the students if anything about the experiment surprised them. Have students think of other experiments that would show how air takes up space. If a suggestion seems applicable, try it out. (This activity was adapted from *Science for the Elementary School*, Victor and Kellough [1994].)

Activity Title: Observe That Air Exerts Pressure

Purpose and Objectives
This demonstration will show students that air exerts pressure equally in all directions.

Materials

- tumbler or plastic glass
- cardboard, or plastic cover from a cottage cheese container
- water

Procedure

Fill a tumbler or plastic glass with water. Place a piece of cardboard or a plastic cover on top of the glass and hold it firmly against the glass with the palm of one hand. Hold the glass over a sink. Grasp the base of the glass with the other hand and quickly turn the glass upside down. Carefully remove the palm of your hand from the cardboard or plastic cover, being careful not to jar the cardboard or the glass. The cardboard and glass will remain in place. Ask the students what happened. (The water stays in place because air is exerting pressure on the cardboard. The pressure of the air against the cardboard is greater than the pressure of the water against the cardboard.) Turn the glass sideways and in many other directions. Have the students note that the water stays in the glass, which shows that air exerts pressure in all directions.

Evaluation, Completion, and/or Follow-up

Invite the students to try the activity for themselves. Encourage students to respond in their journal to the following questions:

1. What happened when you let go of the cover?
2. What happened when you tipped the glass in all directions?
3. What do you think would happen if you used a half-full glass?

Activity Title: Observe That Air Has Weight

Purpose and Objectives

Through this activity students will observe that air—a gas—has weight that can be measured. The students will also experience systems, interactions, and patterns of change.

Materials

- two identical balloons
- meter stick
- scissors
- tape
- string

Procedure

Hang a meter stick evenly from a doorway or other high place. Use a string and tape to secure it so that it acts as a balanced beam. Attach a string loosely to each of the two inflated balloons. (Large, round balloons that are the same size work best. Blow them up so they are the same size when inflated.) Tape each string end to an end of the meter stick. Be sure the stick is level after the balloons are hung. If it is not, place a partly open paper clip on the stick where needed to balance it. Puncture one balloon with a pin. The deflated balloon will not weigh as much as the balloon that still has air in it, and the meter stick will become unbalanced. Note: When the balloon bursts, a piece or two may be blown off. Be sure to collect the pieces and drape them around the balloon. Otherwise the results will be inaccurate.

Evaluation, Completion, and/or Follow-up

Encourage the students to think of other experiments they could try to prove that air has weight. Have the students write their reactions to these properties of air activities in their science and math journal.

Activity Title: Make a Weather Vane

Purpose and Objectives

This activity builds on the previous activities that demonstrated the properties of air—volume and weight. Students will see the force of air against a weather vane that they have constructed. This activity can be used to introduce a unit on meteorology, and to measure and demonstrate the theme of patterns of change.

Materials

- pencil
- clay
- straw
- scissors
- glue
- straight pin
- ruler
- stiff construction paper or oak tag
- square pieces of cardboard
- beads

Procedure

Have the students make their own weather vane. Provide them with the following instructions: Cut two pieces from the construction paper—the head and the tail of the weather vane—for the straw, making sure the tail is much larger than the head. Cut a notch in each end of the straw. Fit and glue the pieces in the notches. Stick a pin through the center of the straw. Wiggle the pin a little to ensure a loose fit, then stick the pin into the eraser end of a pencil, putting a bead between the straw and the eraser so the straw may swing freely. Use a small piece of clay to help balance the straw if needed. Mark the four compass point directions of the weather vane by drawing a vertical and horizontal line (so that they intersect at right angles) on the square piece of cardboard. Mark the four main directions—N, S, E, W—near the edges of the square in the appropriate places. Put a lump of clay in the center of the square. Push the pencil upright into the clay

Instruct the students to go outdoors. Have the students line up the N on their weather vane with north. Have them watch the way their vane points in the wind.

Evaluation, Completion, and/or Follow-up

Have the students try to determine from which direction the wind is blowing. Instruct them to record their guess in their science and math journal, and state why they think their guess is correct. Encourage students to hypothesize what the wind direction will be at different times during the day. Instruct students to keep a record of wind direction for a week. Encourage them to look for patterns and provide their reasoning in their journal. (This activity was adapted from *Science In Elementary Education* [Gega, 1994].)

Activity Title: Design a Thermometer

Purpose and Objectives

Through this experiment students will observe how water expands and contracts as the temperature changes. It will allow students to construct their own tool for measuring this change, and open the door to an understanding of expansion and contraction, meteorology, and the themes of systems, interactions, and patterns of change.

Materials

- water
- red food coloring

- Pyrex flasks
- eyedroppers
- long glass or plastic tubes
- one-hole rubber stoppers
- index card
- a standard thermometer

Procedure
Mix water and red food coloring until the water is a dark red. Instruct students to pour this mixture into a Pyrex flask until the flask is almost full. Have students insert a long glass or plastic tube in a one-hole rubber stopper and fit the stopper tightly into the mouth of the flask. Advise the students that the amount of water in the flask needs to be increased by adding water to the top of the tube with the eyedropper, so that the colored water will rise about one third to one half the distance of the part of the tube that extends above the stopper.

Have the students make two slits in an unlined index card and slide the card over the tube. Fix the card to the tube with tape. Instruct students to mark the original height of the water. Place the flask in a sunny location and allow the water time to warm. Have students observe and mark the change in the water. Then move the flask to a darker, cooler location and allow the water time to cool. Again, have students observe and mark the height of the water. This procedure can be repeated by carefully setting the flask in a pan or bowl with ice and water or by taking it outside if it's cold.

Throughout the activity, have students measure the temperatures with the standard thermometer and compare the results. Show students how they can calibrate their own thermometer by using the readings from the standard thermometer.

Evaluation, Completion, and/or Follow-up
Encourage students to record their calibrations on the scale of the index card and compare them with the readings on a standard thermometer. Have students take daily readings outdoors on a standard thermometer (placed away from direct sunlight) for an extended period of time. Instruct students to keep a record of these readings in their science and math journal. Have students make a chart or a graph showing the changes in temperature during the year. (This activity was adapted from *Science for the Elementary School*, [Victor 1985].)

Activity Title: Understanding and Observing Living and Nonliving Things

Purpose and Objectives

Through this activity students will observe and learn about the different characteristics of living and nonliving things. They will learn that living things have characteristic traits by which they can be described and distinguished from nonliving things. Living things take in nutrients and give off wastes. They grow, reproduce, and respond to stimuli from their environment. All living things need certain resources to grow, such as air or other gases to breathe, water, and food. If any of these resources are lacking, the organism (or living thing) will die. Plants and animals are living things. Nonliving things, by contrast, have none of these characteristics. However, nonliving things do change and transform to the effects of nature.

Materials

- science and math logs
- pencils
- crayons
- markers

Procedure

Discuss with students what they think is living. Encourage them to give examples. Students can readily identify a live object from a nonliving thing. In this activity students will heighten their awareness of the living things all around them. Take the students outdoors to a selected spot on the playground or the school grounds. Have them take along their log, pencils, crayons, and markers, and find a spot away from each other if possible. Once students have found their spot, instruct them to write or draw all the living things they see, such as ants or other insects, grass, and trees, in their science and math log. Have them also write or sketch all the nonliving things they see, such as a flag pole, cement sidewalk, swing, or building.

When students return to the classroom, conduct a discussion about what they saw. Have students exhibit their drawings and compare lists. Develop a class list, on the board or on a large piece of paper, that outlines the characteristics of each item.

Evaluation, Completion, and/or Follow-up

Encourage students to report on the *new* things they observed. Ask students to write in their log what was most surprising to them. Have students explain in their log what they learned by doing this activity. Share drawings with the class.

Activity Title: Describing Living Things: A Thinking Game

Purpose and Objectives
This is a simple guessing game in which children will take turns describing pictures of plants and animals, and having the other students guess the name of the plant or animal.

Materials

- a collection of magazine or newspaper pictures of a wide variety of plants and animals

Procedure
Have one student select a picture from the stack of pictures that the rest of the class cannot see. Have the student describe the picture for the class without identifying the plant or animal by name. Encourage vocabulary used in the science and math classrooms. For example, "I'm thinking of a plant we use for a snack. It is also eaten by birds." Students can then question: Is it a root? Is it a seed? Is it a flower? Creative thinking is encouraged when spontaneous demonstrations of children's intuitive and rational thinking work together.

Evaluation, Completion, and/or Follow-up
Encourage students to save the pictures they have described. Make a master list of the plant and animal life. Use the words for spelling, and talk about the variety of life they found. Young students can take cutouts of plant and animal life and put them where they fit in the environment—like birds in the sky, trees in the forest, and seeds on a plant in a garden. Make mobiles that show different layers of life in the air, on land, and in the sea. Different colors of yarn can be used to hang the different living things according to the ecosystem in which they live.

Activity Title: Looking at Individual Health

Purpose and Objectives
This introductory activity will give students some information about their attitudes, daily health habits, diet, exercise, and other matters concerning their health. It will also provide teachers with a base for discussion about health and wellness.

Materials

- science and math logs
- pencils

Procedure

Brainstorm with the class about what they think are the things that make people healthy. Write their responses on the chalkboard. Divide the class into several teams of four or five students. Assign each team a topic from the following list:

- emotional and mental health
- exercise
- environmental health
- food, nutrition, and eating habits
- relating to others
- relaxing and self-awareness

Encourage each team to discuss their topic and make notes. Have each team select one member to report their findings to the class. Have the class sit in a circle. Have each team representative give a one-minute talk about their group's discussion. Students in the class should take notes in their science and math journal and write down questions.

Evaluation, Completion, and/or Follow-up

Encourage students to consult their science and math log, examine questions, and write down comments on where they think their health can be improved. Evaluate their responses and provide feedback on their opinions and questions on health.

Activity Title: Drawing Maps of the Body

Purpose and Objective

Through this activity students will observe the interconnectedness of the different systems within the human body.

Materials

- a long piece of paper for each student cut from a large roll of paper
- crayons or markers
- paints
- reference books on the human anatomy

Procedure
Explain to students that they are going to make maps of their bodies. Have them pick a partner to trace the outline of their body while they lie on the long sheet of paper. Explain that they will collaborate in teams to fill in the details of one of the following systems of the body:

- skeletal—map the major bones of the body
- digestive—map the esophagus, liver, intestines, mouth, throat, and anus
- circulatory—map the heart, lungs, mouth, throat, major arteries, veins, and kidneys
- brain and nervous system—map the brain, spinal cord, and major nerves

Assemble teams of four students and have each one pick a system on which to work. Present student groups with reference books, models, and charts. Encourage students to use pencil first, before painting or coloring the sytems. Have them use the reference materials. Circulate among the groups while they're working. When the teams are finished, invite all the students to the front of the room for group presentations.

Evaluation, Completion, and/or Follow-up
Encourage students to listen and write down any questions. Allow time for class discussion and questions at the end of student presentations. Put the group projects up around the room and on bulletin boards outside the classroom.

Activity Title: Representing Atoms

Purpose and Objectives
Through this activity students will begin to understand that an atom is the smallest piece of matter. This means that if a piece of matter is continually cut in half, a point would finally be reached where only a single atom remains. Because atoms cannot be seen without special microscopes, this activity will let students look at the small parts of everyday things to get a feeling of what scientists mean when they talk about atoms.

Materials

- sugar cubes
- four-color pictures from magazines
- small pieces of fabric

- hand lenses
- pencils
- science and math journals

Procedure
Have students examine a small portion of one of the pictures with just their eyes. Then have them examine it again with a hand lens. Have students draw or write in their science and math journal about what they observed. Have students examine the fabric with just their eyes, then use the hand lens. Have them record their observations in the science and math journal. Have students examine the sugar cube first without a hand lens, then with it. Instruct them to draw or write a description of what they observed.

Evaluation, Completion, and/or Follow-up
Compare the differences of the items seen without and with the hand lens. Determine from what were the smaller parts of each of the items made, or what they looked like. Speculate what would happen if these items were examined using a microscope—a microscope that could see atoms.

Activity Title: How Hot? How Cold? How Can I Control It?

Purpose and Objectives
Through this activity students will learn about the interrelationships between heat energy and color.

Materials
- one black cloth
- one white cloth
- two pennies
- science and math journals

Procedure
Introduce the activity by explaining to the students that they will explore some of the ways they control their own temperature. Explain the exercise and allow time for discussion. Have the students predict what will happen and record their predictions in their science and math journal.

Have the students place the two pennies on a sunny windowsill. Instruct the students to cover one penny with the black cloth and the other penny with the white cloth. Let the covered pennies sit for about two hours, then remove the cloths. Have the students examine the pennies and write their reactions in their science and math journal.

Evaluation, Completion, and/or Follow-up
Have the students discuss how this experiment applies to the color they wear most often when it is warm or cold outside.

Activity Title: Exploring How Light Travels in a Straight Line

Purpose and Objectives
Through this activity students will observe how light travels in a straight line unless acted on by an outside force.

Materials

- four index cards
- thumbtacks
- four small 3" × 5" blocks of wood
- a flashlight

Procedure
Have the students find the center of the four index cards by drawing diagonals on each card. Instruct the students to make a quarter-size hole at the center of each card. Direct the students to attach a small piece of wood to each card with a thumb tack. Have the students place the index cards in front of each other about two inches apart, making sure that the holes are in a straight line. Have students test their experiment by turning on the flashlight (the students may wish to rest the flashlight on some books so that its pointed directly at the holes in the cards).

Evaluation, Completion, and/or Follow-up
Darken the room and turn on the flashlight. Have the students look through the holes and see the light of the flashlight traveling through the holes in a straight line. Now lightly clap two chalkboard erasers together over the beam so that the students can see the beam of light traveling in a straight line. Encourage the students to write their reactions to this activity in their science and math log. (This activity was adapted from *Science for the Elementary School* [Victor 1985].)

Activity Title: Catch-the-Light Game

Purpose and Objectives
Through this activity students will learn how light, which usually travels in a straight line, can be bent and directed using mirrors.

Materials

- a bright flashlight
- several small mirrors

Procedure

Darken the room except for one bright flashlight. Have one student catch the light from the flashlight and reflect it onto a wall with a small mirror. Have another student catch that spot of light and pass it on. Have the students see how many times they can pass the light (depending, of course, on the strength of the light source and the number of mirrors they have available). Have a student that is toward the beginning of the chain tilt or lower his or her mirror, then put it back. Have another student further along the chain do the same.

Evaluation, Completion, and/or Follow-up

Instruct the students to write the directions for the catch-the-light game. Direct students to include some of their best tricks or ideas for catching and passing. Make a copy of the students' directions and comments. Have the students practice the game again, and then go to another classroom and share it. Encourage students to take the directions home to be shared with their friends and family.

Activity Title: Testing the Speed of Sound

Purpose and Objectives

Through this activity students will observe how sound travels over distance and time.

Materials

- large outdoor space
- a hammer
- a large piece of wood or metal

Procedure

Take the students outside. Have half of the class stand in a long line that stretches out as far as they reasonably can (twenty or thirty feet between each student is ideal). Have the other half stand by and observe. Instruct the students in line to raise their hands when they hear the loud sound. Go twenty or thirty feet from one end of the line and hit the piece of wood or metal sharply with the hammer. Then have the students in line trade places with the students that were observing. Repeat the exercise.

Evaluation, Completion, and/or Follow-up
Have the class come together and discuss their observations. Have the students record the distance and the time they observed the hammer hit the wood in their science and math journal.

Chapter Four

Teaching Mathematics: Engaging Students in Mathematical Inquiry

The right question at the right time can move children to peaks in their thinking that result in significant steps forward and real intellectual excitement.
—Eleanor Duckworth, *Teachers, Teaching and Teacher Education*

Like the discipline of science and its pedagogy, mathematics and mathematical curriculua are in a constant state of flux. Mathematics and science are the parents of technology, constantly challenged to fulfill their voracious appetite for discovery. As this relationship shapes and pushes virtually every aspect of our society—which in turn constantly demands more technology—it comes as no surprise that the mathematics classroom is at the heart of the dynamic: The challenge—and the excitement—therefore, must manifest first in the teacher, who is at the heart of the classroom.

Although the metamorphosis of mathematics spans centuries, most of what affects the classroom today has occurred within the last fifty years. Within that period the need for change has accelerated, creating a demand for formally recognized standards of curriculum application. Then, too, much has happened since the NCTM standards for school mathematics were released in 1989. More attention is now being given to problem solving, cooperative learning, critical thinking, interdisciplinary connections, manipulatives, the use of technological tools, and professional development.

Professional development for teachers is becoming more like that for other fields. It is a continual process that extends from the undergraduate college years to the end of a career. Teachers of mathematics are now vested with decision-making powers, as curricula are changed and resources are allocated. With this providence teachers have a greater opportunity to become leaders, as they decide how to help children learn mathematical concepts and skills, develop positive attitudes toward mathematics and their mathematical abilities, and understand the mathematical connections to the world in which they live.

Children learn mathematics best when they use new ideas, develop new connections, and explore new relationships. The challenge for the teacher is to engage students in meaningful mathematical activities that create a clear inner logic about concepts and applications. By adapting curricular material to meet these needs, teachers can increase and deepen the mathematical understanding of maturing students.

Changes in Mathematics Education

At the beginning of the twentieth century, E. L. Thorndike introduced the stimulus-response theory called *connectionism*. This approach viewed learning as building strong connections, so rote learning was emphasized. Repeated speed and correct answers were accomplished by many drill sessions. Teachers sequenced skills by level of difficulty and taught topics *in order*. Standardized tests were soon developed. Teachers found they needed to drill students even harder to ensure scoring high on the tests.

Until about 1920 it was thought children learned best by training the mind much like athletes build up the strength of their muscles. Mathematics was taught to strengthen mental aptitudes. In the 1920s Dewey reacted to strict, drill-based learning by advocating incidental learning. He felt that children would learn as much as they needed and learn it better if arithmetic were not taught as an abstract concept. The basic idea was to train teachers so that they could help children make mathematical connections to the natural world.

In the late 1950s Americans were surprised and alarmed when the Soviet Union launched the satellite Sputnik into space. This achievement caused the United States to question its competency in science, mathematics, and technology. The United States responded by launching a reform effort in mathematics and science. The *new math* of the late 1950s and 1960s was born.

This new math dealt with content, such as the structure of mathematics, set theory, and number operations and their inverses. Scientists and mathematicians became the primary contributors to the developing mathematics programs for the elementary school. Like the science projects also developed in the 1960s, mathematics was focusing on discovery. New content was added, and the concepts of algebra and geometry were brought to the lower grade levels. Like all systemic changes, some of them worked and some of them didn't. One significant shortcoming was that too little attention was given to the training of teachers. Like much of the public, many teachers did not understand the principles behind this new program. Unfortunately, many of the hopes evoked by these programs were not realized.

In the 1970s, when it became apparent that the promise had not materialized, there was another drastic swing in the curriculum. Rather than build on what had worked in the past while eliminating what hadn't, as other professions do, renewed emphasis was placed on the skills needed for everyday survival. The minimal-competency movement of the 1970s was a swing back to earlier times. Thus, the mathematical skills of addition, subtraction, multiplication, and division were again considered by many to be the prime necessities for children living in a world that was soon to be filled with calculators and computers. The use of scientific skill-based textbooks again was revived.

In the 1980s, educators realized that the developmental level of children was a determining factor in teaching and deciding the sequence of the curriculum. Attention was focused on the evidence that students construct their own understandings based on their experiences. This theory, called *constructivism*, had its roots with ideas expressed by Piaget (1972), Brownell (1935), Bruner (1986), and Dienes (1960). By the 1980s this movement was taking hold and a research base was building to support the first edition of the national mathematics standards in 1989. For the first time there was general agreement and a coherent commitment: Standards didn't mean standardization, and teachers where allowed to perform to the best of their abilities by becoming pedagogical decision makers.

An Overview of the Curriculum and Evaluation Standards for School Mathematics

The *Curriculum and Evaluation Standards for School Mathematics* was first published by the NCTM in 1989. It started the trend toward national subject matter standards. The *Curriculum and Evaluation Standards for School Mathematics* is available from the NCTM, 1906 Association Drive, Reston, VA 22091-1593; (800) 235-7566.

Among many other things, the standards propose that all students

- learn to value mathematics and become more aware of mathematics in their lives
- become more confident in their ability to do mathematics
- become effective problem solvers
- learn to communicate clearly, both mathematically and logically
- recognize mathematical connections and be familiar with the power of technology
- understand and be able to apply mathematical reasoning

The standards also call for a broader scope of mathematics studies. More emphasis is placed on statistics, probability, and practical applications to the world in which children live. The emphasis was shifted from a focus on memorizing formulas and algorithms to making connections between mathematics and the world. The math standards support this idea by suggesting that dealing with problems stemming from a student's natural interests promotes a willingness to persevere until a solution is found.

The NCTM standards for mathematics and problem solving, paraphrased here, are as follows

1. Students will apply mathematics using problem solving to explore and understand mathematical content.
2. Students will generate questions and go on to explore the problems that are associated with those questions within and outside mathematics.
3. Students will develop and apply strategies to solve a wide variety of problems.
4. Students will confirm and interpret problem results.
5. Students will gain confidence in using mathematics meaningfully.

The NCTM standards for mathematical relationships and communication, paraphrased here, are as follows:

1. Students will connect the relationship between physical materials, pictures, and diagrams to mathematical ideas.

2. Students will reflect on and clarify their thinking about mathematical ideas and situations.

3. Students will relate their everyday language to mathematical language and symbols.

4. Students will use the skills of discussing, reading, viewing, writing, and listening to interpret and evaluate mathematical ideas.

5. Students will discuss mathematical ideas, make predictions, and produce convincing arguments.

6. Students will come to appreciate the value of mathematical notation. For example, they should understand that place value and scientific notation are a vital part of learning and using mathematics.

The NCTM standards for mathematical reasoning, paraphrased here, are as follows:

1. Students will use logic in figuring out solutions.

2. Students will use models to make independent investigations and understand basic facts, and use properties and relationships to explain their thinking.

3. Students will justify their answers and solutions, and use patterns and relationships to analyze mathematical situations, to help them believe that mathematics makes sense.

The NCTM standards for applying mathematics and making connections, paraphrased here, are as follows:

1. Students will use their knowledge to take everyday situations and translate them into mathematical representations.

2. Students will relate various mathematical representations of concepts or procedures to real-life situations.

3. Students will recognize relationships among different topics in mathematics.

4. Students will use mathematics in their daily lives.

The NCTM standards for estimation, paraphrased here, are as follows:

1. Students will recognize when an estimate is appropriate.

2. Students will determine the reasonableness of results.

3. Students will apply estimation in working with quantities, measurement, and problem solving.

The NCTM standards for number sense and systems, paraphrased here, are as follows:

1. Students will construct number meanings through real-world experiences using physical materials.
2. Students will understand our number system by relating counting, grouping, and place-value concepts, and developing number sense.
3. Students will interpret the multiple uses of numbers encountered in their daily experiences.
4. Students will understand, represent, and use numbers in a variety of equivalent forms, such as fractions, decimals, integers, and rational numbers.

The NCTM standards for computational skills, paraphrased here, are as follows:

1. Students will develop meanings for the operations by modeling and discussing a rich variety of problem situations.
2. Students will relate mathematical language and symbolism to problem situations, recognize that a wide variety of problem structures can be represented by a single operation, and develop an operation sense.
3. Students will compute with whole numbers, fractions, decimals, integers, and rational numbers.
4. Students will recognize, use, and estimate with percents.
5. Students will model, explain, and develop a reasonable proficiency with basic facts and algorithms.
6. Students will use a variety of mental computational and estimative techniques.
7. Students will use calculators in appropriate computational situations.
8. Students will select and use computational techniques appropriate to specific problems.

The NCTM standards for geometry and spatial sense, paraphrased here, are as follows:

1. Students will describe, model, draw, and classify shapes.
2. Students will investigate and predict results of combining, subdividing, and changing shapes.
3. Students will develop a spatial sense and relate geometric ideas, and number and measurement ideas.

4. Students will recognize and understand the geometric concepts necessary to function effectively in a three-dimensional world.

5. Students will develop and appreciate geometry as a means of describing their world.

6. Students will have a knowledge of concepts such as parallelism, perpendicularity, congruence, similarity, and symmetry.

The NCTM standards for measurements, paraphrased here, are as follows:

1. Students will understand attributes of length, weight, area, volume, time, temperature, and angle.

2. Students will develop the process of measuring, and make and use measurements in problems and everyday situations.

3. Students will learn to calculate simple perimeters, areas, and volumes.

4. Students will be able to measure in both the metric and customary systems.

The NCTM standards for statistics and probability, paraphrased here, are as follows:

1. Students will collect, organize, and describe data.

2. Students will construct, read, and interpret displays of data.

3. Students will formulate and solve problems that involve analyzing data.

4. Students will explore concepts of chance.

5. Students will present information about numerical data such as measures of central tendency (mean, median, mode) and measures of dispersion (range, divination).

6. Students will know how to construct, read, and draw conclusions from simple maps, tables, charts, and graphs.

The NCTM standards for patterns and relationships, including their use in algebra, paraphrased here, are as follows:

1. Students will recognize, describe, expand, and create a wide variety of patterns.

2. Students will represent and talk or write about mathematical relationships.

3. Students will investigate the use of variables and open sentences to express relationships.

4. Students will learn to use and understand variables (letters) to represent quantities in mathematics.

5. Students will represent mathematical relationships and functions using graphs, tables, and equations.

It should be noted that the National Research Council (1989) lent strong support to the standards document with the publication of *Everybody Counts: A Report to the Nation on the Future of Mathematics Education.* The curriculum and evaluation standards were followed up by the publication of *Professional Standards for Teaching Mathematics* (NCTM 1991). The mission of the NCTM is to provide vision and leadership for improving mathematics education. The NCTM also set forth the goal of ensuring that every teacher of mathematics is given the opportunity to grow professionally. The NCTM clearly recognizes the fact that giving all children the opportunity to receive an equitable, standards-based mathematics education means creating collaborative professional development situations in which the best sources of university expertise are linked with the experiences and needs of teachers.

The goals articulated by the standards can be responsive to accelerated changes in our society, our schools, and our classrooms. Individual teachers can make alterations within their classrooms, but the school itself must have a coherent program of mathematical study for students. No curriculum should be carved in stone at any level; rather, it must be responsive to the lessons of the past, the concerns of the present, and the human and technological possibilities of the future.

Mathematics Today

There is little doubt about the traditional discrepancy between school mathematics and mathematical applications in the real world. Actual math problems outside of school have often had little to do with the information found in math textbooks or what is taught in the classroom. The mathematics curriculum is changing to make it more relevant to the content and skills students need to meet changing societal and intellectual demands. Today's schools recognize the need to reform and rethink the mathematics program. Teamwork, critical thinking, problem solving, and active communication are at the core of teaching for mathematical understanding.

There is a great deal of misunderstanding about the topic of mathematics because mathematics is often confused with arithmetic.

Arithmetic focuses on the computational skills of addition, subtraction, multiplication, and division with whole numbers, fractions, and decimals. Mathematics is much more than computation. It embodies methods of thinking that provide us with a way to organize our thoughts, make plans, analyze data, and solve real-world problems. The National Research Council (1995) speaks to the power and importance of today's mathematics curriculum by saying the following:

> Education in any discipline helps students learn to think, but education must also help students take responsibility for their own thoughts. While this objective applies to all subjects, it is particularly apt in mathematics education because mathematics is an area in which even very young children can solve a problem and have confidence that the solution is correct—not because the teacher says it is, but because the inner logic is so clear. (p. 2)

Mathematics is a multidimensional vehicle for discovery, and in a cooperative, inquiry-based classroom, students develop their critical thinking skills, self-confidence, and sense of self-reliance when they come to possess knowledge of the following:

1. Mathematics is an examination of patterns and relationships. Students must recognize the repetition of mathematical concepts and connections among mathematical ideas. These relationships and concepts help unify the math curriculum, as each new concept is interwoven with former ideas. Students quickly see how a new concept is similar or different from others already learned.

2. Mathematics is a tool. Although mathematics is the tool scientists, mathematicians, and technologists use in their work, it is also used by other people every day. Students begin to understand why they are learning the basic facts and concepts that the school curriculum involves. Like mathematicians and scientists, they also use mathematics to solve problems. Students should realize that mathematics is involved in many careers and occupations.

3. Mathematics is an art. Characterized by harmony and internal order, mathematics needs to be appreciated as an art form in which everything is related and interconnected. Art is thought to be subjective. By contrast, objective mathematics is often associated with memorized discrete facts and skills, yet the two

are closely related to each other. As one author explains: Art interprets the visible world, Mathematics and science explain its abstract workings (Shlain 1991, p. 18)

4. Mathematics is a language, a means of communicating. Like any language, mathematics uses terms and symbols to represent information. The language of mathematics enhances our ability to communicate across the disciplines of science, technology, statistics, and of course mathematics.

5. Mathematics is interdisciplinary. Mathematics relates to many subjects: Science and technology are obvious; however, literature, music, art, social studies, physical education, and sports all make use of mathematics in some way.

Learning and Problem Solving

Content information and the characteristics of effective instruction (pedagogy) are equally important to teachers. Pedagogy without content is sterile, and content without pedagogy aborts its image. When the power of both come into play, students learn the subject and the strategies, habits, and meaning of being an empowered learner.

An empowered learner is a creative problem solver and organizer. Some of the qualities displayed by creative problem solvers indicate that they are

- curious and questioning
- eager to figure things out for themselves
- willing to seek out challenges
- able to think things through
- persistent
- resourceful and flexible
- systematic
- independent
- confident
- willing to take risks (Casey and Tucker 1994)

A good mathematics curriculum is so focused on problem solving, organizing, and planning, that associated strategies become second nature (Casey and Tucker 1994). Both the mathematics and the science standards support this idea and suggest that solving problems and thinking critically help students develop their mathematical and their scientific abilities more fully (Harty 1991). Students who understand mathematics can reason and solve problems in and out of school.

Mathematical Power

During the 1990s mathematics became more concerned with making students mathematically powerful (California Department of Education 1992). This means empowering students to think and communicate using mathematical ideas, while drawing on the techniques and tools of mathematics. Students who are mathematically powerful think and use related activities such as analyzing, classifying, planning, comparing, investigating, designing, inferring, and constructing hypotheses. Mathematically powerful students make meaningful connections, construct mathematical models, raise questions, and test and verify them (Silver 1985).

Communication is essential to the coherent expression of one's mathematical processes and results. When children or adults communicate they generally use ideas that make sense to them. Students should be encouraged to express their ideas orally or in writing during the early stages of conceptual development. As teachers of language arts know, talking, listening, reading valuable material, and developing writing process skills can benefit every subject.

Mathematically powerful work is purposeful. It may be motivated by curiosity, whimsy, or need, but it will always seem more significant to the student if it has a sense of purpose. When mathematics places more emphasis on understanding and responding to student interest, experience, and strength, learning is more meaningful and fun. This style of active and extended mathematical inquiry helps make concepts easier to remember, new procedures easier to understand, and enhances problem solving. When power and pleasure combine in a lesson students are more likely to seek new ideas on their own (Skemp 1978). The result of adding such self-direction to the process is more powerful and more enjoyable learning.

Mathematical Inquiry Activities

Activity Title: Math and Science Pattern Search

Purpose and Objectives

Mathematics and science applications are all around us. Mathematical patterns are everywhere. Architecture, art, and everyday objects rely heavily on mathematical principles, patterns, and symmetrical geometric form. Students need to see and apply real-world connections to concepts in science and mathematics. This activity will get students involved and more aware of the mathematical and scientific relationships all around them, and they will use technology to help report their findings. Through this activity students will participate in observing, communicating, and collecting samples; exhibit their understanding by recording their observations in their science and math log; show their ability to work in groups in a responsible, interactive, and productive manner; and reflect their thinking orally and in writing.

Materials

- pencils or pens
- paper or science and math journals

Procedure

Divide the class into four groups. Direct each group to find and list as many objects as they can that meet the requirements on their list. Some objects may need to be sketched if students don't know what they are called. Encourage them to find and list as many things as possible within a time limit of fifteen minutes. Create the search groups as follows:

1. Group one: Measurement search—This group will use the mathematical skills of measuring, comparing, inferring, ordering by distance, and formulating conclusions. This group shall find and list objects that are

   - as wide as their hand and one foot long
   - farther away than they can throw and waist high
   - half the size of a baseball and as long as their arm
   - smaller than their little finger and wider than four people
   - thinner than a shoelace and as wide as their nose

2. Group two: Shape search—This group will use the mathematical skills of comparing shapes, recognizing patterns, and recording data. This group shall find and list objects that have these shapes: triangle, circle, square, diamond, oval, rectangle, and hexagon.

3. Group three: Number pattern search—This group will use the mathematical skills of comparing numbers, shapes, and patterns, and recording data. This group shall find and list objects that show number patterns. For example, a three-leaf clover matches the number pattern three.

4. Group four: Texture search—This group will use the mathematical skills of classifying, recording data, comparing, and labeling. This group shall find and list objects that have the following characteristics: smooth, rough, soft, grooved or ridged, hard, bumpy, furry, sharp, wet, and grainy.

Evaluation, Completion, and/or Follow-up

When students return, have them list their objects in some type of order or classification if they haven't already. Using a graphing program on the computer or colored paper, scissors, glue, and markers, have them visually represent their results in some way (a bar graph, for example) that (1) indicates the amount of items in each category and (2) can be compared to other findings. When these are complete, have a spokesperson from each group talk about their results to the class.

Activity Title: Estimating with a Pumpkin

Purpose and Objectives

Teaching mathematics in the primary grades tries to make numerals an essential part of the classroom experience. Children need many chances to recognize quantities and see relationships between numbers. When learning beginning concepts, children need to investigate by manipulating concrete materials and relating numbers to problem situations. Young students benefit by talking, writing, and hearing what other children think. In the following activity children will be involved in estimating, counting, verbalizing, writing, and comparing as they estimate the size, weight, circumference, and number of seeds of a class pumpkin.

Materials

- one six-pound pumpkin
- small cut-out measuring squares (one-inch)
- a Zip-Lock bag
- a scale
- one three-pound book

- yarn
- scissors
- index cards

Procedure
Place the pumpkin on a table at the front of the room. Make a poster with these questions and room for the students' names and their estimates: *How tall is the pumpkin? How much does the pumpkin weigh? What is the circumference of the pumpkin? How many seeds are in the pumpkin?*

Have students lay out the measuring squares in a line on their desk to estimate how many one-inch squares they think will equal the height of the pumpkin. Direct students to find their name on the poster in the front of the room. Ask them to write their estimate on the poster, then measure the pumpkin using the measurement squares. Ask the students to write their estimate and the final measurement in their science and math journals.

Instruct students to hold the book to feel the weight of three pounds, then have them hold the pumpkin. Ask the students if the pumpkin weighs the same as the book, more, less, or as much as two books and how many pounds would that be. Have students record their estimates on the class chart and in their journal. Then measure how much the pumpkin weighs by putting it on the scale. Have students record the numbers in their journal. Have the students read the estimate chart to see who is the closest.

Take yarn and scissors, and instruct students to cut a strip of yarn to the length they think would go around the pumpkin. Have students measure their yarn with the measurement squares, estimating the number of inches of the circumference of the pumpkin. Direct students to record their estimates on the class chart, then measure the circumference of the pumpkin. Have the students check the chart to compare the accuracy of their figures. Have them write the numbers in their journal.

Have students estimate the number of seeds in the pumpkin and write their numbers on the class chart. Then cut the pumpkin and remove the seeds for the class to count. When the pumpkin is cut and the seeds removed and washed, the class can count the seeds and compare estimates, writing the numbers down in their journal.

Evaluation, Completion, and/or Follow-up
Discuss the activities with the class. Ask students if they can think of other things that can be estimated this way.

Activity Title: Number Sense and Number Systems: Place-Value Activities

Purpose and Objectives

The NCTM standards indicate that "students must understand numbers if they are to make sense of the ways numbers are used in their everyday world . . . and an understanding of place value is crucial" (NCTM, 1989, 38). Place value forms the foundation of the number system. There are four important characteristics of the number system:

1. Place value—The position of a digit represents its value. For example, the digit 2 in the numbers 21, 132, and 213 represents different ways of thinking about the value of the number 2. In the first case, 2 represents two tens, or twenty; the second 2 represents two ones, or two; and in the third case, the 2 represents two hundreds, or two hundred.

2. Base of ten—The word *base* in the number system means a collection. In this number system, ten is the value that determines a new collection. This system has ten digits: 0, 1, 2, 3, 4, 5, 6, 7, 8, and 9. This collection is called a base-ten system.

3. Use of zero—Unlike some other numeration systems, ours, the Hindu Arabic system, has a symbol for zero. Have students think about the Roman numeral system, which has no provision for zero.

4. Additive property—The Hindu Arabic system has a specific way of naming numbers. For example, the number 432 names the number 400 + 30 + 2.

Children in early grades need experience in counting many objects; trading for groups of tens, hundreds, and thousands; and talking together about their findings. Young children need many models. Bean sticks and base-ten blocks are two models widely used by teachers. But students also need piles of materials (rice, beans, straws, counters, and unifix cubes) to practice counting, grouping, and trading. This activity will help them become familiar with the principles of base ten and place value.

Materials

- standard primary classroom math manipulatives
- rice, beans, straws, and so on
- paper
- glue

- scissors
- markers

Procedure
The base-ten system works by trading ten ones for one ten, ten tens for one hundred, ten hundreds for one thousand, or the reverse—trading one ten for ten ones, and so on. In teaching this principle base-ten blocks are a great ready-made model. Encourage students to make their own models. Building models with popsickle sticks and lima beans works equally well, or have students use construction paper and scissors to make their base-ten models by cutting out small squares of paper and pasting them on a ten strip to form a ten. Then after completing ten tens, paste the ten strips together to make a hundred, then paste the hundreds together to form a thousand. It's time-consuming work, but well worth the effort.

It is important that children think of numbers in many ways. A good place to start is to pass out a base-ten mat with the words ones, tens, and hundreds. Also pass out base-ten blocks to each of the students (units, longs, and flats). The units represent ones, longs represent tens, and flats represent hundreds. Now have the students build the number they hear. If, for example, the teacher says the number 42, the students take four long rods (tens) and place them in the tens column of their mat, and two units, placing them in the ones column. Encourage students to test their skill in a small group by thinking of a number, verbalizing it, and then checking other students' mats.

Using the other manipulatives, put several numbers on the board and ask students to duplicate the numbers, grouping by tens as they work. This makes the task of counting easier for children. Counting by tens also helps students check errors in their counting. But most importantly, sorting by tens shows students how large amounts of objects can be organized.

Tell students they are going to invent a new number system. They've chosen the term *zonker* for the new system. The zonker system has the digits 0, 1, 2, 3, and 4. This collection is called a base-zonker system. Give students some unifix cubes. Have them build a zonker. Practice counting to zonker. In the base-ten system, after counting to nine, the next number is ten, and the number after that would be eleven; in the base-zonker system, after counting to four, the next number is zonker, and the number after that would be zonker one, then zonker two, and so on. The counting would continue like this until students reached one zonker and four, and then two zonker. Then have students set up for the zonker place-value activity described in the following paragraph.

Have students make a place-value mat with a sheet of paper. Have them draw a line down the middle of the paper. On the right side of the line, have students write ones; on the left write the word *zonkers*. Have students put four square spaces on each side. Instruct the students that each time they hear you clap they should put one unifix cube in a space on the mat and say what happened. For example, at the first clap students take one unifix cube and place it in the ones column. They read their mat by saying "no zonkers and one"; at the second sound, "no zonkers and two". Keep counting until the group gets to no zonkers and four. At the fifth clap students should reach for another cube, but this time the ones collection is finished. Students need to rearrange the unifix cube collection by stacking the cubes together to make a zonker and moving their collection to the zonkers column. This is read "one zonker and zero". Keep counting and exchanging. Continue the zonker place-value activity. When students reach four zonkers and four, ask if they know what the next number will be. Discuss their suggestions. Then continue so that they will see that the next number becomes zonker, and will continue on and on, like the base-ten system.

Evaluation, Completion, and/or Follow-up

After the zonker activity goes on for a while, stop the class and discuss what they have found. Ask the students to compare the base-ten system with the base-zonker system. Write a two- or three-digit number on the board. Have the students determine what the number represents in base ten and base zonker. Discuss the results. Have them write their results in their journal.

Activity Title: Mathematics as Reasoning: Addition, Subtraction, Multiplication, and Division Using Manipulatives

Purpose and Objectives

Teachers are encouraged to integrate the concrete and the abstract parts of school science and mathematics. A typical elementary classroom has several sets of manipulative materials to improve computational skills and make learning more enjoyable. Base-ten blocks will be used in these activities to describe the sequence of moving from concrete manipulations to the abstract algorithms. Students will become familiar with the blocks, and will discover the vocabulary (ones = units, tens = longs, hundreds = flats) and the relationships among the pieces. Students will explore trading relationships in addition, subtraction, multiplication, and division.

In grades K–4 the mathematics curriculum should include concepts of addition, subtraction, multiplication, and division of whole numbers so that students can

- develop meaning for the operations by modeling and discussing a rich variety of problem situations
- relate the mathematical language and symbolism of operations to problem situations and informal language
- recognize that a wide variety of problem structures can be represented by a single operation
- develop operation sense (NCTM Standard 8: Whole Number Computation)

In grades K–4, the math curriculum should develop whole number computation so that students can

- model, explain, and develop reasonable proficiency with basic facts and algorithms
- use a variety of mental computations and estimation techniques
- select and use computation techniques appropriate to specific problems and determine if the results are reasonable

Materials

- base-ten blocks
- standard classroom fare described in each component

Procedure
This activity contains seven components that build and relate to each other. The evaluation, completion, and/or follow-up information is included in each component when applicable.

Component One: The Banker's Game
In this activity small groups of students will be involved in grouping by tens. Divide the class into small groups of four to five players and one banker. Provide each player with a playing board divided into units, longs, and flats. Explain the use of the board: Any blocks the students receive should be placed on the board in the column that has the same shape at the top. Begin the game by having a student roll a die and ask the banker for the number rolled in units. Have the students place the units column on his or her board. Each child is in charge of checking his or her board to decide if a trade is possible. The trading rule states that no player may have more than nine objects in any column

at the end of their turn. If there are more than nine objects, the player must gather them together and go to the banker and make a trade (for example, ten units for one long). Do not proceed to the next player until all the trades have been made. The winner is the first player to earn five tens. This game can be modified by using two dice and increasing the winning amount.

Component Two: The Tax Collector's Game
This game is simply the reverse of the Banker's Game. The emphasis here is on the regrouping of tens. Players must give back in units to the bank whatever is rolled on the die. Have the children decide before the game begins whether an exact roll is necessary to go out or not. To begin, have all players place the same number of blocks on their boards. Explain that exchanges must be made with the banker. Rules are made quickly by the students (for example, when rolling a six, a player may hand the banker a long and ask for four units back). Instruct students to explain their reasoning to each other. The winner is the first student to have an empty playing board (Suydam and Reys 1978).

Component Three: Making Connections in Addition and Subtraction
When children are learning about the operations of addition and subtraction, it's helpful for them to make connections between these processes and the world around them. Story problems help them see the actions of joining and separating. Use manipulatives and sample word problems to give them experience in joining sets and to help them figure out the differences between them. By pretending and using concrete materials, learning becomes more meaningful.

Component Four: Look for Patterns in Addition Problems
Help students look for patterns within addition problems, such as finding a ten, grouping numbers together, multiplying numbers, or rounding up or down. Ask students for other helpful ways to solve the problem. Have them work with a partner or in a small group. Point out any strategies for adding columns of numbers that are helpful.

Component Five: Teaching Division with Understanding
Base-ten blocks bring understanding to an often complex algorithmic process. The following exercise is a good place to start when introducing division: Using base-ten blocks, have students show 393 with flats, rods, and units. Have the students divide the blocks into three equal piles. Ask students to explain what they did—how many flats in each pile, how many rods, and how many units. Give students several more

problems. For example, start with 435 and have the students divide it into three piles. Encourage students to explain how many flats, rods, and units they found at the end of all their exchanges. In this problem, one flat will have to be exchanged for ten rods (tens), and then the rods divided into three groups—one rod remains. Next, students will have to exchange the one rod for ten units, and then divide the units into three groups. No units are left in this problem. Continue doing more verbal problems, pausing and letting students explain how they solved them. What exchanges were made? It is helpful to have students work together, to explain their reasoning to each other, to correct each other, and to ask questions. After many problems—perhaps in the next class session—explain to the students that they are now ready to record their work on paper, still using the blocks. Then show them two ways to write the problem: $435 \div 3 =$ and $3\overline{)435}$. Then ask them the following three questions and wait until all students have finished with each question:

1. How many hundreds in each group? Have the students look at their record sheet. Above the division symbol of the problem, they should answer one flat, so they should record one on their sheet.

2. How many cubes in all? Have students check how many cubes are represented. They should answer three hundred, so they should record three hundred on their sheet.

3. How many are left? Have students return to the problem and subtract: $435 - 300 = 135$.

Now the problem continues. Start over and ask the following three questions:

1. How many tens in each group? Have students look at their record sheet. Above the division symbol of the problem, they should answer four tens, so they should record four on their sheet.

2. How many tens in all? Have students check how many cubes are represented. They should answer 120, so they should record 120 on their sheet.

3. How many are left? Have students return to the problem and subtract: $135 - 120 = 15$

Now students have arrived at the last stage (the ones). Again, have students answer the following three questions:

1. How many ones in each group? Have students look at their record sheet. Above the division symbol of the problem, they should answer five, so they record five on their sheet.

2. **How many ones in all?** Have students check how many cubes are represented. They should answer 15, and they should record 15 on their sheet.

3. **How many are left?** Have students return to the problem and subtract 15 − 15 = 0. (Burns 1998, *Mathematics with Manipulatives* [videotape]).

For advanced students this seems like an elaborate way of doing division. By using manipulatives and teaching with understanding, beginning division makes sense to elementary students. Teachers can introduce shortcuts later to make more advanced division easier and faster.

Component Six: Real-Life Division Problems
Follow the division exercises with real-life problems. For example, tell students the following story: While walking to school four children found a ten-dollar bill. When they arrived at school, they told the teacher; she asked them to tell the principal. The principal thanked them and told them she would try to find out who lost the money. A week later, the principal called the students back to her office and told them no one had claimed the money, so it was theirs to keep. The children were delighted, but they first had to figure out a way to share it equally among the four of them.

Students work together to solve the problem. Ask them to record their solution and explain their reasoning. Have them write two statements on the board—one that explains the amount of money each person receives and one that justifies their solution.

Component Seven: Student-Generated Problems
Have student groups make up division problems of their own to share with the class. These can be problems that actually happened or they can be invented problems. Be sure students share their solutions and explain their reasoning.

Evaluation, Completion, and/or Follow-up
Included in each component when applicable.

Activity Title: Patterns and Relationships

Purpose and Objectives
Children encounter patterns all the time. Many possibilities in math instruction open up if teachers take a broader view of patterns. Teachers can connect many ideas in mathematics to children's background knowledge by encouraging them to describe patterns and relationships

in their own language to help them represent those ideas with mathematical symbols. For example, if a child has described a pattern such as "each object is three more than the last one," he or she can represent the idea symbolically as n (the object) and describe the nth object as n + 2. Through this it is clear that patterns and relationships naturally lead to an understanding of functions in algebra. In the components that follow, students will explore only a few types of patterns and relationships, and ways to describe them. The more opportunities children have to describe patterns and relationships with pictures, words, tables, and variables, the more power they will have with mathematics.

Materials

- standard classroom fare as described in each component

Procedure

This activity contains two components that build on and relate to each other. The evaluation, completion, and/or follow-up information is included in each component when applicable.

Component One: Multiplication Building Rectangles
Discuss rectangles, demonstrate, and review how to name them (e.g., two-by-three [two rows of three units], four-by-five [four rows of five units]. Provide students with a sheet of graph paper. Have students plan a design, creature, or scene that they can make using only rectangles. Have students cut the graph paper into rectangles, using the whole page, then paste the rectangles onto construction paper to make their design. Have students write a number sentence that tells how many one-by-one rectangles are included in their design. Since all students started with the same size graph paper, they should all get the same answer, although their equations will be different. If the class uses a ten-by-ten graph paper grid, students can write statements that show what percentage of the whole picture is represented by each part. Have students write stories about their pictures. The stories should include mathematical statements.

Component Two: Multiplication Factor Puzzle
Place a large sheet of butcher paper on the board. Divide the paper and label each part with a multiplication product (18, 20, 21, 36, 40, and so on). Divide the class into teams. Ask each team to find and cut out of graph paper all the rectangles that can be made with a given number (20, for example). Have each team label and paste their rectangles on the butcher paper under that number. As a whole class, re-

view the findings and determine if all the possible rectangles have been found for each number without duplicates (flips, rotations). List the factors for each number.

Evaluation, Completion, and/or Follow-up
Included in each component, when applicable.

Activity Title: Statistics

Purpose and Objectives
It is difficult to listen to the news on TV or pick up a newspaper without noticing the extensive use of charts, graphs, probability, and statistics. Using the following components students will learn the elementary concepts of probability and graphing.

Materials

- standard classroom fare described in each component

Procedure
This activity contains six components that build on and relate to each other. The evaluation, completion, and/or follow-up information is included in each component when applicable.

Component One: Classify in Terms of Certain, Uncertain,
Impossible, Likely, and Unlikely
Give students a list of statements and ask them to sort the statements into three piles labeled certain, uncertain, and impossible. Use statements such as the following:

1. Tomorrow it will rain.
2. I will get one hundred percent correct on my next spelling test.
3. Tomorrow we will all visit Mars.
4. If I flip a coin it will either land heads or tails.

As the children classify the statements, discuss with them the reasons for the classifications. When they have finished, ask them to classify further the uncertain statements as either likely or unlikely. Let students turn to activities and experiments to clarify their thinking. As a follow-up activity, have students come up with their own list of statements to classify into categories (Cruikshank & Sheffield 1992).

Component Two: Predicting

Ask students to predict whether a coin will land on heads or tails. Flip the coin and show the result. Ask students to predict the outcome of several flips of the coin. Discuss if one flip seems to have an influence on the next flip. Explain that events are called independent if one event has no effect on another. Give each child a penny and ask them to make a tally of the heads and tails out of ten flips. Talk about such terms as *equally likely, random,* and *unbiased.*

Show the children a spinner with three colors (red, yellow, blue). Spin the spinner a few times to show that it is a fair spinner. Ask students to predict the number of times they could expect to get yellow if they spin the spinner thirty times. Can students find a formula for predicting the number of times a color will come up? If the probability of landing on each color is equally likely, they can write the probability of landing on any one color as the total number of outcomes divided by the number of favorable outcomes.

In the example of the spinner, the total number of outcomes is three because there are three colored sections altogether. Therefore, the probability of getting yellow is one out of three or one third. Ask the children to predict the number of times they could expect to get yellow if they spun the spinner thirty times. Try the experiment using different colors and different numbers of spins.

Component Three: Finding a Random Sample

Discuss with students how they might take a random sample of marbles. A random sample is obtained in such a way that every member of the sample group has an equal chance of being chosen. Put five red and forty-five blue marbles in a bag. Tell students to take a random sample of ten marbles and try to predict the total number of marbles in the bag. Then let them know there are fifty marbles altogether. Discuss their prediction. Ask students: *Would you trust your prediction based on the results of only ten draws? What if you repeated the ten draws several times?*

Component Four: Exploring Sports Statistics with Basketball Averages

The following are the salaries of five professional basketball players: $80,000, $80,000, $100,000, $120,000, and $620,000. The players are complaining about their salaries. They say that the mode of the salaries is $80,000 and that they deserve more money for all the games they play. The owners claim the mean salary is $200,000 and that this is plenty for any team. Which side is correct? Is anyone lying? How can students explain the difference in the reports?

Ask students to look in newspapers and magazines for reported averages. Are there any discrepancies in the reports? Bring in reports for discussion in class. Encourage students to read any reported statistics carefully.

Component Five: Graphing with Young Children
The concepts of graphing can be learned as early as kindergarten, and children should graph data frequently in the early grades. Graphs, tables, and charts are often used to display data and communicate findings. Instruct students to bring their favorite stuffed bear to school. As a class, sort the bears in various ways—size, color, type, and so on. Graph the results with the class. Have students sort the bears in another way and paste paper counters or stickers on paper to make their own personalized graph.

Component Six: Surveying, Collecting Data, and Graphing
Divide the class into small groups of four or five. Have students brainstorm about what they would like to find out from the other class members (favorite hobbies, TV shows, kinds of pets, and so forth). Once a topic is agreed on and approved by you, have them organize and take a survey of all class members. Remember several groups will be doing this at once, so allow for some noise and movement. When the statistics are gathered and compiled, have each group make a clear, descriptive graph that can be posted in the classroom. Encourage originality and creativity.

Evaluation, Completion, and/or Follow-up
Included in each component, when applicable.

Activity Title: Fractions and Computation

Purpose and Objectives
Fraction concepts are among the most complicated and important mathematical ideas that students encounter. Perhaps because of their complexity, fractions are also among the least understood by students. Some of the difficulties may arise from the different ways of representing fractions: spoken symbols, written symbols, manipulative materials, pictures, and real-world situations. It's difficult for students to make sense of these five ways of representing fractions and to translate them in meaningful ways.

Students need many chances to work with concrete materials, observe and talk about fractional parts, and relate their experiences to scientific and mathematical notation. One helpful activity is to have students make a fraction kit. This introductory activity will introduce fractions to students. Fractions are presented as parts of a whole.

Materials

- seven different 3 × 18 in. strips of colored construction paper
- a pair of scissors for each student
- envelopes to hold the set of fraction pieces labeled as follows: 1, ½, ⅓, ¼, ⅛, ¹⁄₁₂, and ¹⁄₁₆ in.

Procedure

Direct students to cut and label the strips as follows: Start by having students select a colored strip. Emphasize that this strip represents one whole. Have students label the strip ¹⁄₁ or 1. Next, ask students to choose another color, fold it in half, cut it, and then label each piece ½. Talk about what one half means (one half means one piece out of two total pieces). Then have students select another color. Have them fold and cut it into four pieces, and label each piece ¼. Again discuss what one quarter means (one piece out of four total pieces). Compare the four pieces with the one whole piece. Continue having students fold, cut, and label a fourth colored strip into eighths, a fifth strip into twelfths, and a sixth strip into sixteenths.

Now each student has a fraction kit. Encourage students to compare the sizes of the pieces and talk together about what they discover. For example, students can easily observe that the fractional piece ¹⁄₁₆ is smaller than the piece marked ¼. This is a good time to introduce equivalent fractions, such as: *How many one-sixteenth pieces would it take to equal one quarter? What other fractional pieces would equal one quarter?* Explaining equivalence with a fraction kit makes fractions more meaningful.

Evaluation, Completion, and/or Follow-up

This follow-up section contains four components that engage students in the use of the fraction kit.

Component One: Fraction Cover-Up

Have students work in small groups. Have each student start with the 1 strip. Using the pieces from the fraction kit, challenge students to be the first to cover the whole strip completely. The game rules are as follows: Have students take turns rolling the cube labeled with fractions. The fraction that is shown when the cube is rolled tells the students the size of the piece to place on their strip. When getting close to the end, students must roll exactly the fraction that is needed.

Component Two: Fraction Equivalence Game

This game gives students opportunities to work with equivalent fractions. Each player starts with the 1 strip covered with two $\frac{1}{2}$ fraction pieces. The challenge is to be the first to remove the pieces completely. Encourage students to follow these rules: Students take turns rolling the fraction cube. A student has three options on each turn: to remove a piece (only if he or she has a piece the size indicated by the fraction on the cube), to exchange any of the pieces left for equivalent pieces, or to do nothing and pass the cube to the next player. A student may not remove a piece and trade on the same turn, but can choose to do one or the other. It is important for students to check each other's trades accurately.

Ask students to cover their 1 piece with whatever smaller pieces they choose. Record examples on the board. For example, if a child chose three one-quarter pieces and two one-eighth pieces, record $\frac{1}{4} + \frac{1}{4} + \frac{1}{4} + \frac{1}{8} + \frac{1}{8} = 1$. Explain how to shorten the equation by counting the fourths and writing $\frac{3}{4}$, then counting the eighths and writing $\frac{2}{8}$: $\frac{3}{4} + \frac{2}{8} = 1$. Encourage students to help shorten other students' recordings on the board. Then have them each cover their strip with at least five different combinations of pieces, and record them on a work page with and without shortening their lists. Have students exchange and check each other's papers.

Component Three: Fraction Kit Sentences

Present students with incomplete fraction sentences. Have them use their fraction kits to complete them. Encourage students to explain orally and in writing why their selections make sense (Burns 1992). There are several variations on this activity:

1. Have students write other fractions that are equivalent to the fraction presented.
2. Present pairs of fractions and have students write >, <, or = to make a true sentence.
3. Ask students to supply the missing fractional number to make the fractions equivalent.
4. Have students discover a way to write one fraction to complete a sentence. They can use their fraction kits for this by covering the problem with all the pieces the same size, so the length can be represented with one fraction.

Component Four: Problem Solving Using Fractions

The following are several examples of using problem-solving situations to make fractions more understandable. Have students explain their thinking. Correct any misconceptions. Invite students to come up with some related problems of their own.

1. Susan has a half of a pizza. She invites a friend over to share it. Show how much pizza Susan has now.

2. Sam has bought a roll of wire from a record store. Now he plans to hook up his stereo, tape player, and VCR. If the roll is 5 feet long, draw a diagram showing how much wire he will use for each item.

3. Have students design some fraction problems to share with others.

Chapter Five

Educational Technology: Engaging Students in Technological Inquiry

As long as there have been people, there has always been technology. Indeed, the techniques of shaping tools are taken as the chief evidence of the beginning of human culture. . . . In the broadest sense, technology extends our abilities to change the world.
—Rutherford and Ahlgren, *Science for All Americans*

Technology has forged its link with science and has become a powerful force in the development of civilization. It is now an intrinsic part of all cultural and educational systems. No school or classroom has remain untouched by the insidious nature of technology: Administrators cannot ignore its presence or expense; teachers cannot deny their students access and training. To this end, the mathematics and science standards now indicate that both high tech (computers) and low tech (simple manipulatives) are essential to inquiry in science and problem solving in mathematics and science. Technology shapes and reflects the values found in society. At school it can isolate learners or help them join with others. Science, mathematics, and technology are reciprocal—each domain helps drive the other. It is important, however, to inject a dose of healthy skepticism into the debate.

Although some of the benefits are undeniable, it takes more than technology to improve instruction or reform American education. Like mathematical and scientific discovery, most technological progress is incremental. Spectacular new approaches and theories are rare events, and will continue to be so. There is no substitute for teacher preparation, curricular content, and classroom application.

Technology is a double-edged sword: It can be an excellent tool for investigation, analysis, inquiry, and problem solving; it can also turn science and mathematics into a spectator sport, or distract learners and destroy classroom momentum by bogging the curriculum down with errant software and time-wasting computer functions and results.

Computers provide an excellent example of how technology can be introduced and promoted in our schools before many teachers have a clear understanding of how to use it, what might be accomplished by using it, and what the benefits might be. Since the early 1980s, schools have been caught between aggressive marketing, technological myths, and promising possibilities. Inservice training and software evaluation were neglected—even though the key to success turned out to be the quality of the software and the way teachers integrated technological tools into their classrooms. How should teachers use computer technology? The new national standards for science and mathematics suggest active, inquiry-based, hands-on learning that uses the computer as a powerful tool for such things as visually exploring models and simulations, and problem solving. There is more to integrating a technological tool such as the computer into the classroom than a manufacturer's sales team would have school administrators and teachers believe.

People often uncritically accept the parameters of computer programs—even when the simulated environment is very wrong. Multimedia compounds the problem of uncritical consumers and users: Technology can have a distancing and solipsistic effect on youngsters who grow up with television, computers, and video games. Simply being motivated by a computer program, for example, doesn't mean that students are learning something important.

In our new media-fed society, images can engage public attention with small controversies and banalities. However, this same media-connected world can also provide students with the possibility of controlling and charting the course of their education and their culture. Information is not constructed and used by a small, elite group but by anyone with a computer, camcorder, or television. The best of the new technology moves students out of a passive realm and toward interaction with others. Technological tools allow students to take control and observe phenomena that would remain otherwise unobservable.

Educational technology is changing how science and mathematics are taught, by changing the instructional environment and providing opportunities for students to create new knowledge for themselves. Computer-based technology can serve as a vehicle for discovery-based classrooms, giving students access to data, experiences with simulations, and the possibility for creating models of fundamental scientific and mathematical technological processes. Electronic learning has many elements: Computers, multimedia, information networks, camcorders, satellite dishes, virtual reality, and television make up just a partial list. Electronic media are transforming our social and educational environments before we have a chance to think carefully about why we want to use the technology and what we hope to accomplish with it.

The Standards and Technology

The scientific and the math standards view technology as helping to form connections between the natural and man-made worlds. Both suggest paying attention to technological design and to how technology can help students understand larger themes and concepts of science and mathematics. The standards suggest that in the elementary grades students should be given opportunities to use technology to explore and design solutions to problems. In addition, the standards suggest themes that help students see human factors and the societal implications. The laws of the physical and biological universe are seen as integral to understanding how technological objects and systems work. The standards also point to the importance of connecting students to the various elements of our technologically intensive world so that they can construct models and solve problems with technology.

The problem-solving ability of children can be developed by first-hand experiences in which they use technological tools similar to those used by scientists, mathematicians, and engineers. Computers and the Internet are important, but students should also see the technological products and systems found in the relatively low-tech world of zippers, can openers, and telephones. Young children can engage in projects that are appropriately challenging for them; projects in which they may design ways to fasten, move, or communicate more effectively. Students begin to understand the design process as well as improve their ability to solve simple problems. In the course of solving any problem for which they are trying to meet certain criteria, students will find elements of science, mathematics, and technology that can be powerful aids. Many lessons can include examples of technological achievement in which science has played a part and can also allow students to examine where technical advances have contributed directly to scientific progress.

Many curricular programs suggest that teachers should integrate science, technology, and societal issues, and present a multidisciplinary analysis of problems that are relevant to the students' world. A sequence of five stages is usually involved in the technology-based, problem-solving process:

1. Identify and state the problem.
2. Designing an approach to solve the problem.
3. Implement and arrive at a solution.
4. Evaluate results.
5. Communicate the problem, design, and solution (National Research Council 1995).

In keeping with the standards document, teachers may also have elementary students design problems and technological investigations that incorporate several interesting issues in science and mathematics. By using a variety of materials and technologies for scientific inquiry and mathematical problem solving, students can come to recognize—as John Dewey has suggested—that education is more than preparing for life; it is life itself.

Using Multimedia Technology to Open Doors for Learning

To be valuable, educational technology must contribute to the improvement of education. Technological tools should help open doors to understanding and provide a setting for reflection—making important points that might otherwise go unnoticed.

The term *multimedia* usually refers to computer programs that use the CD-ROM medium to incorporate large amounts of text, graphics, video clips, and stereo sound. Most desktop personal computers now come with built-in CD-ROM drives. For those that do not, an external drive can usually be connected to a computer. Video and CD-ROM disks provide a random access feature that allows users to move quickly to the part of the program they wish to view.

The interactive design of new multimedia programs is support-ing the findings regarding cognitive development and collaborative learning. Computer-based activities can have problem-centered structures that wrap learning experiences around problems in new ways. As budding scientists, students can use computer tools to ex-plore visually empirical claims and examine all kinds of evidence, allowing them to support or critique important findings within sci-ence and mathematics. As state-of-the-art pedagogy is connected with state-of-the-art technological tools, it will change the way knowledge is constructed, stored, and learned.

The benefits of multimedia technology do not come without a caveat. Studies confirm that the power and permanency of what students learn is greater when visually based mental models are used in conjunction with the printed word. Inferences drawn from visual models can lead to more profound thinking (Dorr 1986). However, students learn to rely on their perceptual (visual) learning even if their conceptual knowledge contradicts it. Even when it runs contrary to verbal explanations or personal experience, the video screen can provide potent visual experiences that push view-ers to accept what is presented.

How to Choose Computer Software

Choosing computer and multimedia software has become an impor-tant part of curricular planning and development. Administrators and teachers must make careful, informed decisions to maximize the benefits of these electronic teaching tools, while protecting students from the frustration and distraction of poorly conceived, ill-written, and pedagogically vapid software marketed to naive consumers un-der the pretense of being beneficial to students. Choosing any soft-ware is not easy; choosing educational software can be a difficult thing to do. Budgetary restrictions add to the difficulty, as educators must wade through heaps of high-tech garbage to find software that will provide their students with effective electronic resources.

Most teachers subscribe to a number of professional journals, and just about every school staff room has dozens of them. The jour-nals are simple enough to give to upper grade students so that they can help with software selection. Many contain software reviews that keep you up to date. Magazines like *Electronic Learning* pub-lish an annotated list featuring what their critics take to be the best new programs of the year. Many older, popular programs have been improved and put on CD-ROM. District supervisors of science and mathematics often have lists of software designed for use at various grade levels. Teachers can involve their classes in the software evaluation process. This allows students to be part of the process, while exposing them to the educational purpose of the activity. As teachers and students go about choosing programs for the classroom, the following checklist may prove useful:

1. Can the software be used easily by two students working together?
2. Does the software feature graphic and spoken instructions?
3. What is the program trying to teach and how does it fit into the curriculum?
4. Does the software encourage students to experiment and think creatively about what they are doing?
5. Is the program lively and interesting?
6. Does it allow students to collaborate, explore, and laugh?
7. Is the software technically sophisticated enough to build on multisensory ways of learning?
8. Is there any way to assess student performance?
9. What activities, materials, or manipulatives would extend the skills taught by this program?

The bottom line in evaluating any software program is: *Do you and your students like it?* We suggest that teachers reserve their final judgment until they observe students using the program. Do not expect perfection. If the software does not build on the unique capacities of the computer, then you may just have an expensive electronic workbook that will not be of much use to anybody. With today's interactive multimedia programs there is every reason to expect science and math programs that invite students to interact with creatures and phenomena from the biological and physical universe. Students can move from the past to the future and actively inquire about everything from experiments with dangerous substances to simulated interaction with long-dead scientists.

Changing Media Symbol Systems

Print and video (or film) take different approaches to communicating meaning. Print relies on the reader's ability to interpret abstract symbols. The video screen is more direct. In both cases thinking and learning are based on internal symbolic representations and the mental interpretation of those symbols. The impact of either medium can be amplified by the other.

Because electronic symbol systems play such a central role in modern communication, they cannot be ignored. It is important that students begin to develop the skills necessary for interpreting and processing all kinds of video screen messages. Symbolically different presentations of media vary as to the mental skills of processing they require. Each individual learns to use a medium's symbolic forms for purposes of internal representation (Bianculli 1992). To even begin to read, a child needs to understand thought-symbol relationships. To move beneath the surface of video imagery requires much of the same understanding. It takes skill to break free from an effortless wash of images and electronically induced visual quicksand.

Unlike direct experience, print or visual representations are always coded within a symbol system. Learning to understand that system cultivates the mental skills necessary for gathering and assimilating internal representations. Whether students spend twenty-five hours a week watching television at home or five hours a week in front of computers at school, the video screen is changing the texture of learning.

Each communications medium makes use of its own distinctive technology for gathering, encoding, sorting, and conveying its contents associated with different situations. The technological mode of a medium affects the interaction with its users—just as the method for transmitting content affects the knowledge acquired. Learning seems to be affected more by what is delivered than by the delivery system itself. In other words, the quality of the programming and the level of interaction are the keys. But different media are more than alternative routes to the same end. Studies suggest that specific media attributes call on different sets of mental skills, and by doing so cater to different learning styles (Solomon 1986).

Processing must always take place, and this process always requires skill. The closer the match between the way information is presented and the way it can be mentally represented, the easier it is to learn. Better communication means easier processing and more transfer. Early on, research suggested that voluntary attention and the formation of ideas can be facilitated by electronic media—with concepts becoming part of the child's repertoire (Brown 1994). Now new educational choices are being laid open by electronic technologies. Many schools already offer courses on the Internet and a few of them grant undergraduate and graduate degrees to cyberstudents. Some educators are skeptical, however. They do not think cyberschools will ever catch on. Over the years, they point out one new technology after another has had bold predictions of educational reform that inevitably floundered. As Larry Cuban, a professor of education at Stanford University argues: "The virtual university concept has echoes of instructional television. Both ideas came out of the impulse to somehow increase the productivity and reduce the cost of traditional education" (Lohr 1996, p. 1).

Understanding and employing these technological forces requires a reasoned view that interprets new literacies from a unique and critical perspective. We would do well to remember that while certain educational principles remained constant, each step along the way—from speech to handwritten manuscripts to computer print—required major changes in teaching and learning.

Understanding and Creating Electronic Messages

Understanding the conventions of visual electronic media can help cultivate mental tools of thought. In any medium this allows the viewer new ways of handling and exploring the world. The ability to interpret the action and messages on a video display terminal requires going beyond the surface, to understanding the deep structure of the medium. Understanding the practical and philosophical nuances of a medium moves its consumers in the direction of mastery.

Seeing an image does not automatically ensure learning from it. The levels of knowledge and skill that children bring with them to the viewing situation determine the areas of knowledge and skill development acquired. Just as with reading print, decoding visual stimuli and learning from visual images requires practice. Students can be guided in decoding and looking critically at what they view. One technique is to have students read the image on various levels. Students identify individual elements, classify them into various categories, and then relate the whole to their own experiences. They can then draw inferences and create new concepts from what they have learned. Many students can now videotape their own scenes with a camcorder, edit their work, and use the family VCR for playback. These new video pencils can transform the landscape of student visual creations.

Planning, visualizing, and developing a production allows students to sort out and use electronic media critically to relay meaning. Young multimedia or video producers should be encouraged to open their eyes to the world and visually experience what's out there. By realizing in the medium, students learn to redefine space and time. They also learn to use media attributes such as structure, sound, lighting, color, pacing, and imaging. Lightweight camcorders and programs like Hyperstudio have made video photography and multimedia production much easier and more accessible. By writing in such a medium students can gain a powerful framework for evaluating, controlling, and creating in electronic media.

Understanding the Symbol Systems of the Future

Since the field of education seems to be entering a unique period of introspection, self-doubt, and great expectations, theoretical guidelines are needed as much as specific methods. To give teachers the freedom to reach educational goals means knowing what those goals are. It is dangerous to function in a vacuum because rituals can spring up that are worse than those drained away. As electronic learning devices flood our schools and homes we need to be sure that findings are linked to practice. A close connection between these two domains requires defining educational needs in a more theoretical and practical way. If the two are not integrated, then one will get in the way of the other.

A wide range of intellectual tools can help students understand social and physical reality. Technology can be an ally in the learning process or it can be an instrument to subvert human productivity and integrity. To avoid the latter, adults and children need to have control over the technology they are using. Research suggests that for students to write well they need to read good literature, understand and practice the research process, write for an actual reader, tap into their personal experiences, and edit their material cooperatively. Learning about electronic communications technology can follow a similar pattern.

Reaching students requires opening students' eyes to things they might not have thought of on their own. This means tapping into real experience, fantasies, and personal visions, with technological tools serving as capable collaborators. The combination of thoughtful strategies and the enabling features of video tools can achieve more lasting cognitive change and improved performance (Riel 1989). With this mind-eye approach, previously obscure concepts can become comprehensible, with greater depth, at an earlier age.

Print, the written word, and hand-drawn pictures (the oldest technological media) have been the cognitive tools western culture has traditionally chosen to use to teach children. Good theoretical and practical techniques, developed for understanding how a traditional communications medium interacts with human learning, will be helpful in understanding the new media—even after we have gone beyond the current technological horizons in education. As print, computers, and video merge, children and young adults can develop explicit metacognitive strategies as they search for data, solve problems, and graphically simulate their way through multiple levels of abstraction.

The Internet and Access to the World of Ideas

As society assembles the technological components that provide access to an individualized set of active learning experiences, it is important to develop a modern philosophy of teaching, learning, and social equity. While new educational communications technology has the potential to make society more equal, it has the opposite effect if access is limited to those with the means to afford the equipment. As society becomes immersed in the world of computers, camcorders, interactive TV, satellite technology, and data bases, schools are often behind the curve and find themselves trying to catch up with the more technologically sophisticated.

Electronically connecting the human mind to global information resources will result in a shift in human consciousness similar to the change that occurred when society moved from an oral to a written culture. The challenge is to make sure that this information is available for all in a twenty-first-century version of the public library.

There is general agreement that we need a reimagining of public education. As Americans try to fix their schools, they find many conflicting proposals and movement in many directions. One of the more popular directions suggests linking the public schools to the Internet. Today more than half the nation's schools already have at least one connection to the Internet. With richer suburban school districts leading the way, this translates into about ten percent of American classrooms having direct access. This is more than three times as many Internet links as in late 1994. What the schools actually do with these connections has not always been figured out. The question that administrators, librarians, and teachers must ask is: *Where will this resource lead and what will it accomplish?*

Will learning on-line become an enormous boon or an enormous bane for education? Caught between promise and misplaced technological enthusiasm, schools and teachers are under pressure from both sides of the argument. Those who propose connecting classrooms to the Internet suggest that it will give students access to an incredible array of learning tools. Opponents say that the new technology promotes trivial pursuits rather than disciplined learning. Skeptics argue that the Internet will distract children from learning—while fans counter by pointing out how it can expand and enrich the way many subjects are taught. Both groups agree that students should learn to use their minds well, communicate effectively, and grow as social beings, but the role of the Internet is constantly in dispute.

Despite the mixed feelings toward the Internet, there are studies that indicate potential benefits when students and teachers use new computer-based technology and information networks:

1. Computer-based simulations and laboratories can be downloaded and help support national standards, especially in math and science, by involving students in active, inquiry-based learning (Dwyer 1994).

2. Technology and telecommunications can help include students with a wide range of disabilities in regular classrooms (Woronov 1994).

3. The Internet may help teachers continue to learn, while sharing problems and solutions with colleagues around the world (Adams and Hamm 1996).

By using the Internet and World Wide Web for distributed learning, educational institutions, companies, and government agencies can deliver information and training to students worldwide in less time and at a lower cost. Children at school can tap into this rapidly evolving technological environment and use simulations to explore electronically time, space, insights, and falsehoods in every corner of the planet.

These benefits notwithstanding, there are drawbacks to incorporating the Internet into the classroom. Since the Internet is rarely censored, it is important to supervise student work or use a program that blocks adult content. Teachers should keep an eye on what students are doing and make sure that the classroom is off-line when a substitute teacher is in. A program like Internet Nanny is a way to prevent children from accessing inappropriate material.

The Internet, like other electronic media, can distract students from direct interaction with peers, inhibiting important group, literacy, and physical activities. Good use of any learning tool depends on the strength and capacity of teachers. The best results occur when informed educators are driving change, rather than the technology itself. If linking the classroom to the Internet is going to have positive results, teachers need a clear set of educational priorities before they select the technologies to advance those priorities. In addition, teachers need training to harness the technology properly for instructional purposes. In recognition of this fact, the National Educational Goals project recognizes the need for "the nation's teaching force to have access to continual improvement of their professional skills" (National Education Goals Panel 1994, p. 3). The notion that positive things happen by simply putting the technology in the classrooms and connecting to the Internet is wrong: The technology only helps children learn better if it is part of an overall learning strategy. As technological potential and hazard collide and intrude on our schools, there is general agreement that teachers need high-tech, inservice training to deal with the explosion of electronic possibility.

> Computer-mediated instruction and communication is just a tool to enhance the teaching learning process. Computers in the classroom will never replace competent and caring teachers or provide an ideal substitute for face-to-face interaction. Learning is context dependent and socially constructed.
>
> Computers in education and everyday communication will dominate life in the 21st century. It is in this spirit of hope and excitement with what the future holds for us that we should incorporate the newest technology into our teaching and learning experiences.

—Susana M. Sotillo

Connecting Students to a Changing Technological World

Science helps drive technology and technology returns the favor. Technology expands as science and mathematics call for more sophisticated instrumentation and techniques to study phenomena that are unobservable by other means due to danger, quantity, speed, size or distance. As technology provides tools for investigations of the natural world it expands scientific knowledge beyond preset boundaries. The students' natural world is not neatly divided up into disciplines—teachers can use technological help to soften calcified subject matter boundaries. The appropriate technological instruments can help teachers with cross-disciplinary themes, while engaging students in a study of the physical and biological universe.

Teamwork and technology are keys to the 21st century. They have the potential to transform the educational process. Connecting these domains to science and mathematics instruction have been major themes in educational reform documents from the *National Education Goals Report* to the *National Science Education Standards*. The new spirit in science and mathematics education supports the link between the collaborative study of subject matter and the cooperative use of technology for interdisciplinary inquiry. Of course neither cooperative learning nor educational technology is *the* answer to our educational problems. But they will help if we can avoid educational delusions about magic bullets.

Technology has consequences—but rarely those that are expected or hoped for, and never only those. Productively dealing with the multifaceted ambiguities of change requires critical thinkers who can work collaboratively. Getting students ever more isolated in front of a computer screen is not a good way to help them become future citizens who can live and work productively. We all need to know when to turn off the computer and interact with live human beings. Going to school means interacting with others and forming relationships with people. It is how those personal interactions are handled that determines the degree to which learning takes place. But there is no inherent reason why communications media and information technology cannot be used to help students accomplish shared goals. And what they learn together they can perform in groups or alone.

A common element in successful classes and successful schools is a shared vision and a socially integrating sense of purpose. Still, movement in new educational directions is more of a journey than it is following a blueprint. As neutral instruments in human hands there is no reason why communications media and cooperative teams cannot become positive parts of a new and larger educational canvas. Both can open doors to more personalized and interactive learning—altering how we learn, work, play, and live. We might just as well be optimistic and assume that at certain intervals reforms arise and new ideas, supported by social forces and new technologies, suddenly change the face of the world for the better.

Technological Inquiry Activities

Activity Title: Egg-Catching Contest

Purpose and Objectives
This is an example of a design activity which meets the science/mathematics/technology standards. Students will design and test a container that can keep a raw egg from breaking when dropped from the ceiling (about 8 ft.).

Materials

- soft packing materials such as: styrofoam peanuts, cotton, paper towers, bubble-wrap
- creative devices such as jello pudding, water, containers, pillow, and so on
- Have students bring in materials from home to meet their group's design plans.

Procedures
This technology activity should be preceded by a unit on force and motion so that students are able to apply their knowledge of science and mathematics in their design process. Divide the class into groups of about four students each. Explain that each group is responsible for planning their egg-catching design. Emphasize creativity. The egg catcher must be 12 inches off the floor.

Explain the problem or challenge. Your group must work together to:

- brainstorm ideas
- sketch a design
- formulate a rationale
- assign group tasks—including clean-up crew
- get materials
- build the container
- try several tests
- perform a class demonstration

Evaluation, Completion, and/or Follow-up
The presentation will begin with a discussion of what each group has done to meet the challenge. Assessment for the egg catcher is not whether the egg broke, but how the students were able to share what they found as they tried to solve the problem and prepared for a success-

ful attempt. It is helpful to have the class make a video of the presentation. It can be viewed again by the designers, by parents, or used in other class sessions in years to come.

Other follow technology activities might include:

- design a device to keep pencils from rolling off your desk
- create something that's easy to make that tastes good and would fit in your lunch box
- design a device that would shield your eyes from the sun
- create an instrument that would make lifting easier
- design ways to save money on school supplies

Activity Title: Communications Time Line

The ways in which people communicate have changed throughout history. In ancient days, cave painting conveyed messages and created meaning for people. For centuries, storytelling and oral language served as the primary means of communicating information. Handwritten manuscripts were the first written form of communication, followed more recently by the printing press, telegraph, telephone, television, typewriter, computer, photocopy and FAX machines, radio, and television.

Purpose and Objectives

Through this activity, students will research the history of communications technology and create a timeline in their science/mathematics journal. This activity allows students to collect as many actual objects as possible or their representations for display. They will provide a written explanation about these communications devices and talk and share their ideas with others, answering any questions the class raises.

Materials

- reference books
- science/mathematics journal
- communication devices from home, grandparents, community, or elsewhere

Procedure

1. Have students conduct research on the history of communications technology and create a timeline. Have them put their notes in their science/mathematics journal.

2. Encourage students to assemble a communications timeline project for display, using as many actual objects or their representations as possible.

3. Remind students that each time period needs to have some examples of the actual objects used and a written explanation about these communications devices.

Evaluation, Extension

1. Direct students to choose a communications technique from the past. Teachers may wish to divide students into groups according to interests and assign each group a certain time period or technological tool used for communication.

2. Direct groups to orally (and perhaps graphically) present their communication tool to the class.

3. Teachers may extend the project by having students project what communications of the future will look like.

Activity Title: Create a Water Clock

Time is often a difficult concept for children to grasp. People have recorded the passage of time throughout history.

Purpose and Objectives

This activity involves children in time measurement using a number of technological tools—past and present. Students will learn how to measure time using a variety of clocks.

Materials

- variety of large cans, plastic bottles, and plastic containers
- a collection of corks or plugs
- modeling clay
- scissors or knife
- hammer and nail with a large head
- science/mathematics journal

Procedure

Have children collect a variety of large cans, plastic bottles, and plastic containers. You may wish to help them make a small hole in the bottom of the metal containers with either a hammer and large nail or in the plastic containers using a scissors or a knife (try to make all of the holes in the containers the same size). Instruct students to make a clay plug or a small cork to fit the hole. Have students fill the containers with water, then release the plugs and compare the times of each container. Encourage students to guess which one will empty first.

Evaluation, Follow-up
Have students choose common jobs that can be timed with water clocks. Encourage students to make a list of things that can be timed with a water clock. Instruct students to hypothesize what the effect of different-sized holes is on the water drip process. Have students use a digital clock to determine how much water flows out in one minute's time from their water clock. Ask students to design a system to mark their water clock to determine the time without measuring the water each time. Ask students if they can make a clock another way.

Follow-up Questions
Instruct students to respond to these questions in their science/math journal:

- Why are clocks so important to the industrial age?
- How are clocks used as metaphors?
- Encourage students to speculate on the future of clocks and their role in the future.

Activity Title: Science Hypothesis Testing

This technology-awareness activity is design to get students involved in the historic role of technology in today's society.

Purpose and Objectives
Students will conduct inquiry in trying to discover what technological devices are being presented. Students will reinforce their skills of questioning, observing, communicating, and making inferences.

Materials
Instruct students to bring in a paper bag containing:

- one item that no one would be able to recognize (an old tool of their grandfather's, for example)
- one item that some people may be able to identify
- one common item that everyone would recognize

Procedure

1. Divide students into small groups. Tell students that all items in their bags should be kept secret.
2. Give the students the following directions:
   A. There is no taking in the first part of this activity.
   B. You are to exchange bags with someone else in your group.
   C. You may then open the bag, remove one item, and write down what you think that item is. Have students examine each item carefully. Also have students write their reaction to how they feel about this item, what they think it may be used for, and which category this item falls into (common item, one some may know, or an item no one would recognize).
3. Repeat with each of the items in your bag.
4. Exchange bags with other groups and go through the same procedure.

Evaluation, Completion, and/or Follow-up

When everyone has finished examining their bag of articles and written their responses, meet back together in your group and explain what you have discovered in your bag. Encourage class speculation, questions, and guesses about unidentified items. The student who brought the unknown tool or article in should be responsible for answering the questions posed, but not give away the identity until all guesses and hypotheses have been raised.

Activity Title: Making Sense of Television

Decoding visual stimuli and learning from visual images require practice. Seeing an image does not automatically ensure learning from it. Students must be guided in decoding and looking critically at what they view.

Purpose and Objectives

This activity will help students critically view what they watch. One technique is to have students "read" the image on various levels.

Procedure

Encourage students to look at the plot and story line. Identify the message of the program. What symbols (camera techniques, motion sequences, setting, lighting, etc.) does the program use to make its message? What does the director do to arouse audience emotion and participation in the story? What metaphors and symbols are used?

- Have students identify individual scenes of the plot (or story)
- Classify the scenes into various categories
- Encourage students to explain their categories by offering evidence of their choices

Evaluation, Follow-up
Instruct students to relate the entire plot to their own experiences, drawing inferences and creating new conceptualizations from what they have learned.

Activity Title: Compare Print and Video Messages

Have students follow a current event on the evening news (taped segment on a VCR) and compare it to the same event as written in a major newspaper.

Purpose and Objectives
Student groups will view news releases on television and in newspapers. Students will discuss print and video messages, comparing and analyzing news content and providing evidence for conclusions reached.

Materials
Have several major newspapers available for each student group and a taped news segment from a major television station (one for each group).

Procedure
Present students with a list of questions for discussion:

- How do the major newspapers influence what appears on a national network's news program?
- What are the reasons behind the different presentations of a similar event?

Encourage comparisons between both media. What are the strengths and weaknesses of each? Instruct groups to provide evidence for their conclusions.

Evaluation, Extension Ideas
Have student groups either write an opinion piece on the news article from the newspaper or a review on the TV newscast.

Activity Title: Extending Our Vision

Our sense of sight can be enhanced by technology that brings objects closer or magnifies tiny objects so they're large enough to see. Our sight can also be enlarged by slowing events so that the action becomes clearly evident. New technologies, such as video cameras, are finding their way into the hands of students and having an impact on their learning. This activity uses a camcorder to extend our vision and accomplish this objective.

Purpose and Objectives

Students will observe and take notes of an experiment that happens before their eyes. Then the experiment will be repeated, only this time it will be taped on a camcorder, slowed down, and shown again. Students will record each event and analyze and manipulate the video tape.

Procedure

1. Instruct students to watch carefully while a classmate pops a balloon filled with water. Conduct a brainstorming session and have students list their observations. Discuss their observations.

2. Inflate a second water balloon. Place the balloon in front of a camcorder mounted on a tripod. Videotape the second balloon as it is popped. Play the video for the students frame-by-frame. Encourage students to describe what happened as the second balloon was punctured by the pin. *Ask students to respond to these questions:*

   A. What happens when a balloon bursts in slow motion?

   B. What things do you observe on the video that you don't see with your unaided eye?

   C. How does technology assist us in observing events like this?

Evaluation, Follow-up

Have students consider how people interpret what they see and hear. Sights and sounds are usually experienced together. Present this as a follow-up activity. Imagine you are a movie director filming an episode of a popping water balloon. Explain how you would do it.

Bibliography

Activities to Integrate Mathematics and Science (AIMS). 1987. *Glide into Winter with Math and Science.* Fresno, CA: AIMS Education Foundation.

Adams, D., and M. Hamm. 1989. *Media and Literacy.* Springfield, IL: Charles Thomas.

———. 1996. *Cooperative Learning.* Springfield, IL: Charles Thomas.

Adams, D., H. Carlson, and M. Hamm. 1990. *Cooperative Learning and Educational Media.* Englewood Cliffs, NJ: Educational Technology Publications.

American Association for the Advancement of Science. 1990. *Science for All Americans.* Washington, DC: American Association for the Advancement of Science.

Anderson, H. 1993. *Toward Teaching 2000: Examining Science Reform.* Presented at the Carleton Lecture, First Annual Convention of the National Science Teachers Association, Kansas City, KS.

Anderson, L., and R. Burns. 1989. *Research in the Classroom: The Study of Teachers, Teaching, and Instruction.* Oxford: Paramon.

Anderson, R., ed. 1993. *Computers in American Schools: 1992: An Overview.* Minneapolis: University of Minnesota, Department of Sociology.

Association for Supervision and Curriculum Development (ASCD). 1994. *Performance Assessment Using the Dimensions of Learning Model.* Alexandria, VA: ASCD.

Atwood, M. 1988. *Cat's Eye.* New York: Doubleday.

Bagdikian, B. H. 1987. *The Media Monopoly.* Boston, MA: Beacon Press.

Bailey, J. 1996. *After Thought: The Computer Challenge to Human Intelligence.* New York: Basic Books.

Barba, R. 1995. *Science in the Multicultural Classroom.* Needham Heights, MA: Allyn and Bacon.

Baron, J. 1988. *Thinking and Deciding.* New York: Cambridge University Press.

Bassarear, T., and N. Davidson. 1992. "The Use of Small Group Learning Situations in Mathematics Instruction as a Tool to Develop Thinking." In *Enhancing Thinking Through Cooperative Learning,* eds. N. Davidson and T. Worsham. New York: Teachers College Press.

Berkeley Holistic Health Center. 1985. *The Berkeley Holistic Health Handbook.* Berkeley, CA: Berkeley Holistic Health Center.

Berlin, D., and A. White 1994. "The Berlin-White Integrated Science and Mathematics Model." *School Science and Mathematics* 94 (1): 2–4.

Berman, L., F. Hultgam, D. Lee, M. Rivkin, and J. Roderick. 1991. *Toward a Curriculum for Being.* Albany: State University of New York Press.

Bianculli, D. 1992. *Taking Television Seriously.* New York: Continuum.

Billiards. For information contact C. Whitney, Science Education Department, Center for Astrophysics, Harvard University, Cambridge, MA 02138; e-mail whitney@cfa.harvard.edu.

Birkerts, S. 1995. *The Gutenburg Elegies: The Fate of Reading in an Electronic Age.* New York: Faber and Faber.

Boomer, G. 1988. *Negotiating the Curriculum.* Busingstake, UK: Falmer Press.

Branley, F. M. 1987. *The Noon Seems to Change.* New York: Thomas Y. Crowell.

Brown, A. 1994. "An Advancement of Learning." *Educational Researcher* 23 (8): 4–12.

Brownell, W. 1935. "Psychological Considerations in the Learning and Teaching of Arithmetic." In *The Teaching of Arithmetic Tenth Yearbook*, ed. W. D. Reeves. Reston, VA: National Council of Teachers of Mathematics.

Bruner, J. 1986. *Actual Minds, Possible Worlds.* Cambridge, MA: Harvard University Press.

Bruner, J., and H. Haste. 1987. *Making Sense: A Child's Construction of the World.* New York: Methuen.

Brussell, E. E., ed. 1970. *The Dictionary of Quoteable Definitions.* Englewood Cliffs, NJ: Prentice Hall.

Bryant, J., and D. R. Anderson, eds. 1988. *Children's Understanding of Television: Research on Attention and Comprehension.* San Diego, CA: Academic Press.

Bulmahn, B., and D. Young. 1982. "On the Transmission of Mathematics Anxiety." *Arithmetic Teacher* 30: 155–156.

Burke, J. 1994. "I Teach English Not Science." *Educational Leadership* 48 (3): 85.

Burns, M. 1991. *Math By All Means.* White Plains, NY: Cuisenaire Company of America.

———. 1988. *Mathematics with Manipulatives.* White Plains, NY: Cuisenaire Company of America (six videotapes) (800) 237-3142.

———. 1992. *About Teaching Mathematics: A K–8 Resource.* White Plains, NY: Cuisenaire Company of America.

Bybee, R. W., and G. E. DeBoer. 1994. "Research on Goals for the Science Curriculum." In *Handbook of Research in Science Teaching and Learning*, ed. D. Gable. New York: Macmillan.

California Department of Education. 1990. *Science Framework.* Sacramento: California Department of Education.

———. 1992. *California Mathematics Framework.* Sacramento: California Department of Education.

Casey, M. B., and E. C. Tucker. 1994. "Problem-Centered Classrooms: Creating Lifelong Learners." *Phi Delta Kappan* 76 (2): 139–143.

Clarke, J., R. Weidman, and S. Eadie. 1990. *Together We Learn.* Toronto: Prentice Hall.

Clement, J. 1983. "A Conceptual Model Discussed by Galileo and Used Intuitively by Physics Students." In *Mental Models,* eds. D. Gentner and A. L. Stevens. Hillsdale, NJ: Lawrence Erlbaum Associates.

Clewell, B. C. 1987. "What Works and Why: Research and Theoretical Bases of Intervention Programs in Mathematics and Science for Minority and Female Students." In *This Year in School Science 1987: Students and Science Learning,* eds. A. B. Champagne and E. L. Hornig, 95–135. Washington, DC: American Association for the Advancement of Science.

Cohen, E. G., R. Lotan, and L. Catanzarite. 1990. "Treating Status Problems in the Cooperative Classroom." In *Cooperative Learning: Theory and Research,* ed. S. Sharan, 203–229. New York: Praeger.

Council of Chief State School Officers. 1994. *Annual Report.* Washington, DC: Council of Chief State School Officers.

Cruikshank, D. E., and L. Sheffield. 1992. *Teaching and Learning Elementary and Middle-School Mathematics.* New York: Macmillan.

Csikszentmihalyi, M. 1996. *Creativity: Flow and the Psychology of Discovery and Invention.* New York: HarperCollins.

Cuban, L. 1994. "Neoprogressive Visions and Organizational Realities." In *Visions for the Use of Computers in Classroom Instruction: Symposium and Response.* Cambridge, MA: Harvard Educational Review Reprint: Harvard Graduate School of Education.

Davidson, N., ed. 1990. *Cooperative Learning in Mathematics: A Handbook for Teachers.* Menlo Park, CA: Addison Wesley.

DeAvila, E., E. G. Cohen, and J. Intill. 1981. *Multicultural Improvement of Cognitive Ability. Executive Summary to the California State Department of Education* (9372). Sacramento, CA: CA Department of Education.

Dede, C. J. 1985. "Assessing the Potential of Educational Information Utilities." *Library Hi-Tech* 3 (4): 115–119.

Dienes, Z. 1960. *Building Up Mathematics.* London: Hutchinson Education.

Dissanayake, E. 1992. *Homo Aestheticus.* New York: Free Press.

Dixon-Krauss, L. 1996. *Vygotsky in the Classroom: Mediated Literacy Instruction and Assessment.* White Plains, NY: Longman.

Dorr, A. 1986. *Television and Children.* London: Sage.

Duckworth, E. 1987. *The Having of Wonderful Ideas and Other Essays on Teaching and Learning.* New York: Teachers College Press.

Duckworth, E. 1987. "Teaching as Research." In M. Okazawa-Rey, J. Anderson, and R. Traver, eds. *Teachers, Teaching and Teacher Education.* Cambridge, MA: Harvard Educational Review.

Dwyer, D. 1994. "Apple Classrooms of Tomorrow: What We've Learned." *Educational Leadership* 51 (7): 4–10.

Eamon, W. 1994. *Books of Secrets in Medieval and Early Modern Culture.* Princeton, NJ: Princeton University Press.

Esler, W., and M. Esler. 1993. *Teaching Elementary Science.* 6th ed. Belmont, CA: Wadsworth.

Farr, R. 1990. "Trends: Setting Directions for Language Arts Portfolios." *Educational Leadership* 48 (3): 103.

Fields, S. 1988. "Cooperative Learning: A Strategy for All Students." *Science Scope* 12 (3): 12–14.

Frederick, A., and D. Cheesebrough. 1993. *Teaching Mathematics.* New York: HarperCollins.

Friedl, A. 1991. *Teaching Science to Children: An Integrated Approach.* New York: McGraw-Hill.

Gallas, K. 1994. *The Languages of Learning: How Children Talk, Write, Dance, Draw, and Sing Their Understanding of the World.* New York: Teachers College Press.

Gardner, H. 1982. *Art, Mind, and Brain: A Cognitive Approach to Creativity.* New York: Basic Books.

———. 1983. *Frames of Mind.* New York: Basic Books.

———. 1987. "Developing the Spectrum of Human Intelligences." *Harvard Educational Review* 57: 187–193.

———. 1990. *To Open Minds.* New York: Basic Books.

———. 1991. *The Unschooled Mind.* New York: Basic Books.

———. 1993. *Creating Minds.* New York: Basic Books.

Gega, P. 1991. *Concepts and Experiences in Elementary School Science.* 7th ed. New York: Macmillan.

———. 1994. *Science in Elementary Education.* 7th ed. New York: Macmillan.

Good, T., and J. Brophy. 1994. *Looking in Classrooms.* 6th ed. New York: HarperCollins.

Graves, D. 1983. *Writing: Teachers and Children at Work.* Portsmouth, NH: Heinemann.

———. 1994. *A Fresh Look at Writing.* Portsmouth, NH: Heinemann.

Gross, J. 1994. "In School: A School Mixing Math, Science, and Minority Students Has Impressive Early Results." *The New York Times*, 3 August, B-7.

Hamm, M. 1992. "Achieving Scientific Literacy Through a Curriculum Connected with Mathematics and Technology." *School Science and Mathematics* 92 (1): 6–9.

———. 1993. "Scientific Literacy: Extending Connections Through Science, Mathematics, and Technology." *School of Education Review* Spring: 62–67.

Hamm, M., and D. Adams. 1992. *Collaborative Dimensions of Learning.* Norwood, NJ: Ablex.

Harris, L., et al. 1994. *Science Literacy Survey.* New York: American Museum of Natural History.

Harty, H. 1991. "Science Problem Solving Approaches in Elementary Classrooms." *School Science and Mathematics* 91 (1): 10–14.

Harvard Graduate School of Education. 1996. "KQED San Francisco, KET Lexington Educational Television Programming." In *Education Bulletin.* Cambridge, MA: Harvard Graduate School of Education.

Hazen, R. 1991. "My Turn: Why My Kids Hate Science." *Newsweek* 2–25.

Heddens, J., and W. Speer. 1994. *Today's Mathematics.* New York: Macmillan.

Hendricksen, B., and T. Morgan, eds. 1990. *Reorientations: Critical Theories and Pedagogies.* Champagne IL: University of Illinois Press.

Henzel Associates. 1996. *Educational Telecommunications: The State-by-State Analysis.* Syracuse, NY: Henzel Associates.

Horgan, J. 1996. *The End of Science: Facing the Limits of Knowledge in the Twilight of the Scientific Age.* New York: Helix/Addison Wesley.

Howe, A., and L. Jones. 1993. *Engaging Children in Science.* New York: Merrill.

James, W. 1909. "The Confidences of a Psychological Researcher." *American Magazine* 68, p. 589.

Katter, E. 1994. "Art and Identity: In Search of Self and Connections with Others." *School Arts* 94 (1): 8.

Kellough, R., J. Cangelosi, A. Colette, E. Chiapetta, R. Souviney, L. Trowbridge, and R. Bybee. 1996. *Integrating Mathematics and Science for Intermediate and Middle-School Teachers.* Englewood Cliffs, NJ: Merrill.

Kidder, T. 1989. *Among Schoolchildren.* New York: Houghton Mifflin.

Kroker, A., and M. Weinstein. 1995. *Data Trash: The Theory of the Virtual Class.* New York: St. Martin's Press.

Lehman, J. 1994. "Integrating Science and Mathematics: Perceptions of Preservice and Practicing Teachers." *School Science and Mathematics* 94 (2): 58–64.

Leitzel, J. 1991. *A Call for Change: Recommendations for the Mathematical Preparation of Teachers of Mathematics.* Reston, VA: Mathematical Association of America.

Levine, M., and R. Trachman, eds. 1988. *American Business and the Public School: Case Studies of Corporate Involvement in Public Education.* New York: Teachers College Press.

Lewis, P. 1996. "Adventures Can Find Company on the Internet." *The New York Times,* 2 July.

LHS GEMS Great Explorations in Math and Science. 1986. *Earth, Moon, and Stars.* Berkeley: University of California Lawrence Hall of Science.

Lohr, S. 1996. "When the Alma Mater Ends With 'Edu'." *The New York Times,* 7 July.

Lonning, R., and T. DeFranco. 1994. "Development and Implementation of an Integrated Mathematics/Science Preservice Elementary Methods Course." *School Science and Mathematics* 94 (1): 18–25.

Maili, G., and A. Howe. 1979. "Development of Earth and Gravity Concepts Among Nepali Children." *Science Education* 63 (5): 685–691.

Martinello, M., and G. Cook. 1994. *Interdisciplinary Inquiry in Teaching and Learning.* New York: Macmillan.

Marzano, R., R. Brandt, C. Hughes, B. Jones, B. Presssein, S. Rankin, and C. Suhor. 1988. *Dimensions of Thinking: A Framework for Curriculum and Instruction.* Alexandria, VA: Association for Supervision and Curriculum Development.

Mathematical Sciences Education Board and the National Research Council. 1990. *Reshaping School Mathematics: A Philosophy and Framework for Curriculum.* Washington, DC: National Academy Press.

McKibben, B. 1992. *The Age of Missing Information*. New York: Random House.

McLeod, J. M. 1982. *Television and Behavior: Ten Years of Scientific Progress*. Vol. 2. Washington, DC: Department of Health and Human Services/United States Government Printing Office.

Mechling, K. R., and D. L. Oliver. 1983. *Handbook 1: Science Teaches Basic Skills*. Washington DC: National Science Teachers Association.

Mumme, J. 1990. *Portfolio Assessment in Mathematics*. Santa Barbara: California Mathematics Project, University of California. CA: NCTM (National Council of Teachers of Mathematics).

National Academy of Sciences. 1996. *National Science Education Standards*. Washington, DC: National Academy Press.

National Art Education Associates. 1992. *Elementary Art Programs: A Guide for Administrators*. Reston, VA: National Art Education Association.

National Assessment of Educational Progress. 1983. *The Third National Mathematics Assessment: Results, Trends, and Issues*. Denver, CO: Education Commission of the States.

———. 1995. *The Third National Mathematics Assessment: Results, Trends, and Issues*. Washington, DC: United States Publications.

National Commission on Testing and Public Policy. 1990. *From Gatekeeper to Gateway: Transforming Testing in America*. Chestnut Hill, MA: National Commission on Testing and Public Policy.

National Council of Teachers of Mathematics (NCTM). *Curriculum and Evaluation Standards for School Mathematics Addenda Series K–6*. VA:NCTM.

National Council of Teachers of Mathematics (NCTM) Commission of Standards for School Mathematics. 1989. *Curriculum and Evaluation Standards for School Mathematics*. Reston, VA: NCTM.

———. 1991. *Professional Standards for Teaching Mathematics*. Reston, VA: NCTM.

National Council of Teachers of Mathematics. 1991. *Curriculum and Evaluation Standards for School Mathematics: Addenda Series K–8*. Reston, VA: NCTM.

———. 1995. *Assessment Standards for School Mathematics*. Reston, VA: NCTM.

National Education Goals Panel. 1994. *The National Education Goals Report 1993: Building a Nation of Learners*. Washington, DC: National Education Goals Panel.

National Research Council. 1989. *Everybody Counts: A Report to the Nation on the Future of Mathematics Education*. Washington, DC: National Academy of Science.

———. 1995. *National Science Education Standards*. Washington, DC: National Academy Press.

National Science Foundation. 1996. *Homeless in the Universe*. Washington, DC: National Science Foundation.

———. (1996) *Shaping the Future*. Washington, DC: National Science Foundation.

National Science Teacher's Association. 1996. *NSTA Pathways to the Science Standards.* Arlington, VA: NSTA.

National Standards for Education in the Arts. 1994. *The Arts and Education Reform Goals 2000.* Washington, DC: United States Office of Education.

Newman, D. 1993. *Experiencing Elementary Science.* Belmont, CA: Wadsworth.

Newmann, F. 1990. "Qualities of Thoughtful Social Studies Classes: An Empirical Profile." *Journal of Curriculum Studies* 22: 253–275.

Newmann, F., ed. 1992. *Student Engagement and Achievement in American Secondary Schools.* New York: College Press.

Northwest Equals. 1989. *Family Science.* Portland, OR: CA Department of Education.

Oliver, M. 1992. "A Summer Day" from *House of Light.* In *New and Selected Poems.* Boston, MA: Beacon Press.

Paterson, I. 1994. "Catching the Flutter of a Falling Leaf." In *Science News* J. Miller, B. Potter eds. Washington, DC: Science Service Publication.

Paulos, J. 1988. *Innumeracy: Mathematical Illiteracy and Its Consequences.* New York: Hill and Wang.

_____ . 1989. *Innumeracy.* New York: Hill and Wang.

_____ . 1992. *Beyond Numeracy.* New York: Vintage Books.

_____ . 1996. "Dangerous Abstractions." *New York Times,* 7 April, Op-Ed.

Pea, R. 1992. "Distributed Multimedia Learning Environments: Why and How." *Interactive Learning Environments* 2 (2): 73–109.

Perkins, D. N., and R. Simmons. 1988. "Patterns of Misunderstandings: An Integrative Model of Misconceptions in Science, Mathematics, and Programming." *Review of Educational Research* 58 (3): 303–326.

Piaget, J. 1972. *To Understand Is to Invent.* New York: Grossman.

_____ . 1973. *To Understand Is to Invent: The Future of Education.* New York: Grossman.

Quinta, F., and B. McKenna. 1991. *Alternatives To Standardized Testing.* Washington, DC: National Education Association.

Raloff, J. 1995. "When Science and Beliefs Collide." *Science News* 149: 360–361.

Ramirez, M., and A. Castanada. 1994. *Cognitive Strategy Research: Educational Applications.* New York: Springer-Verlag.

RelLab. Distributed by Academic Software Library, Box 8202, North Carolina. State U. Raleigh, NC 2769–8202; 800-955-TASI.

Resnick, L. B., and L. Klopfer. 1989. *Toward the Thinking Curriculum: Current Cognitive Research.* Alexandria, VA: ASCD Publishing.

Reys, R. E., M. N. Suydam, and M. M. Lindquist. 1989. *Helping Children Learn Mathematics.* Englewood Cliffs, NJ: Prentice Hall.

_____ . 1992. *Helping Children Learn Mathematics.* 3rd ed. Boston, MA: Allyn and Bacon.

_____ . 1995. *Helping Children Learn Mathematics.* 4th ed. Boston, MA: Allyn and Bacon.

Riel, M. 1989. "The Impact of Computers in Classrooms." *Journal of Research on Computing in Education* 22: 180–190.

Rutherford, F. J., and A. Ahlgren. 1990. *Science for All Americans*. New York: Oxford University Press.

Sagan, C. 1994. *Pale Blue Dot*. New York: Random House.

Sanders, M. 1994. "Technological Problem-Solving Activities as a Means of Instruction: The TSM Integration Program." *School Science and Mathematics* 94 (1): 36–43.

Savage, J. 1994. *Teaching Reading: Using Literature*. Madison, WI: Brown and Benchmark.

Schiller, F. 1954. *Aesthetic Education of Man*. New Haven, CT: Yale University Press.

Schneps, M. 1988. *A Private Universe*. Santa Monica, CA: Pyramid Film and Video.

Sclove, R. 1996. *Democracy and Technology*. New York: Guilford Press.

Sears, J., and J. D. Marshall. 1990. *Teaching About Curriculum*. New York: Teachers College Press.

Segal, J. W., S. F. Chipman, and R. Glaser, eds. 1985. *Thinking and Learning Skills*. New York: Teachers College Press.

Shamos, M. 1995. *The Myth of Scientific Literacy*. New Brunswick, NJ: Rutgers University Press.

Sharan, S., and R. Shachar. 1988. *Language Learning in the Cooperative Classroom*. New York: Springer-Verlag.

Shelton, M. 1994. "Leaf Pals." *Science and Children* 32 (1): 37–39.

Shlain, L. 1992. *Art and Physics: Parallel Visions of Space, Time, and Light*. New York: Morrow.

Shoenfeld, A. 1985. *Mathematical Problem Solving*. Orlando, FL: Academic Press.

Sigler, R. S. 1985. *Children's Thinking*. Englewood Cliffs, NJ: Prentice Hall.

Silver, E., ed. 1985. "Research on Teaching Mathematical Problem Solving: Some Under-Represented Themes." In *Teaching and Learning Mathematical Problem Solving: Multiple Research Perspectives*. Hillsdale, NJ: Lawrence Erlbaum Associates.

Skemp, R. 1978. "Relational Understanding and Instrumental Understanding." *Arithmetic Teacher* 26 (3): 9–15.

Slavin, R. E. 1989. *School and Classroom Organization*. Hillsdale, NJ: Lawrence Erlbaum Associates.

————. 1990. *Cooperative Learning: Theory, Research, and Practice*. Englewood Cliffs, NJ: Prentice Hall.

Smolin, L. 1997. *The Life of the Cosmos*. New York, NY: Oxford University Press.

Snauwaert, D. T. 1993. *Democracy, Education, and Governance: A Developmental Conception*. Albany: State University of New York Press.

Solomon, C. 1986. *Computer Environments for Children: A Reflection on Theories of Learning and Education*. Cambridge, MA: MIT Press.

Sotillo, S. M. 1997. "English-as-a-Second-Language Learning and Collaboration in Cyberspace." Unpublished paper, Montclair State University.

Stasson, M. F., T. Kameda, C. D. Parks, S. K. Zimmerman, and J. H. David. 1991. "Effects of Assigned Group Consensus Requirement on Group

Problem Solving and Group Members' Learning." *Social Psychology* 54 (1): 25–35.

Steinberg, L., et al. 1996. *Beyond the Classroom: Why School Reform Has Failed and What Parents Need to Do.* New York: Simon and Schuster.

Steinberg, L., B. Brown, and S. Dornbusch. 1996. *Beyond the Classroom.* New York: Simon and Schuster.

Stenmark, J. K. 1989. *Assessment Alternatives in Mathematics: An Overview of Assessment Techniques That Promote Learning.* Berkeley: University of California Lawrence Hall of Science. (Prepared by the EQUALS staff and the Assessment Committee of the California Mathematics Council Campaign for Mathematics. For information, contact EQUALS, Lawrence Hall of Science, University of California, Berkeley, CA 94720.)

Sternberg, R., and R. Wagner. 1986. *Practical Intelligence: Nature and Origins of Competence in the Everyday World.* New York: Cambridge University Press.

Suydam, M., and R. Reys. 1978. *Developing Computational Skills: 1978 Yearbook National Council of Teachers of Mathematics.* Reston, VA: National Council of Teachers of Mathematics.

TEAMS. 1994. Downey, CA: Los Angeles County Office of Education.

Templeton, S. 1991. *Teaching the Integrated Language Arts.* Boston, MA: Houghton Mifflin.

Tinker, B. 1991. *Thinking About Science.* Cambridge, MA: Harvard University Press.

Tobin, K. G. 1990. "Research on Science Laboratory Activities: In Pursuit of Better Questions and Answers to Improve Learning." *School Science and Mathematics* 90 (5): 403–418.

Tobin, K. G., D. Tippins, and K. Hook. 1992. *Critical Reform of the Science Curriculum: A Journey from Objectivism to Constructivism.* Paper presented at the National Association for Research in Science Teaching, Boston, MA.

Tolman, M., and G. Hardy. 1995. *Discovering Elementary Science.* Boston, MA: Allyn and Bacon.

Trafton, P. R., ed. 1989. *New Directions for Elementary School Mathematics.* Reston, VA: NCTM.

Van De Walle, J. A. 1994. *Elementary School Mathematics: Teaching Developmentally.* 2nd ed. White Plains, NY: Longman.

Victor, E. 1985. *Science for the Elementary School.* 6th ed. New York: Macmillan.

Victor, E., and R. Kellough. 1994. *Science for the Elementary School.* 7th ed. New York: Macmillan.

Vygotsky, L. S. 1962. *Thought and Language.* Cambridge, MA: MIT Press.

Watson, S. B. 1991. "Cooperative Learning and Group Educational Modules: Effects on Cognitive Achievements." *Journal of Research in Science Teaching* 28 (2): 141–418.

Western Regional Environmental Education Council. 1986. *Project Wild Boulder.* Boulder, CO: Western Regional Environmental Education Council.

Westley, J. 1988. *Constructions.* Sunnyvale, CA: Creative Publications.

White, E. M. 1985. *Teaching and Assessing Writing.* San Francisco, CA: Jossey-Bass.

White, R., and R. Gunstone. 1992. *Probing Understanding.* Bristle, PA: Falmer Press.

Whyte, D. 1994. *The Heart Aroused.* New York: Currency Doubleday.

Wiggins, G. 1989."Creating a Thought Provoking Curriculum." *American Educator* 70: 703–713.

————. 1989. "A True Test: Toward More Equitable Assessment." *Phi Delta Kappan* 70: 703–713.

Willis, S. 1990. "Transforming the Test: Experts Press for New Focus on Student Assessment." In *ASCD Update 1.*

Woronov, T. 1994. "Assistive Technology for Literacy Produces Impressive Results for the Disabled." *The Harvard Education Letter* X (5): 6–7.

Zillman, D., ed. 1992. *Media, Children, and the Family: Social Scientific, Psychodynamic, and Clinical Perspectives.* Hillsdale, NJ: Lawrence Erlbaum Associates.

Index